ONE WAY TICKET

Birgit Ohms

 FriesenPress

Suite 300 - 990 Fort St
Victoria, BC, V8V 3K2
Canada

www.friesenpress.com

Copyright © 2019 by Birgit Ohms
First Edition — 2019

Additional Contributions by Cynthia Reyes

ISBN
978-1-5255-5300-4 (Hardcover)
978-1-5255-5301-1 (Paperback)
978-1-5255-5302-8 (eBook)

1. Family & Relationships, Abuse, Domestic Partner Abuse

Distributed to the trade by The Ingram Book Company

ONE WAY TICKET

CHAPTER 1

ON MY WAY

My hair was in disarray. The wind was strong, and I stood leaning over the railing, looking at the wild waves that the boat was cutting through the water. The ride was only a couple of hours, and I thought I could almost see land. I was leaving home for Munich, Germany.

Mamma had traveled with me from Stockholm to Copenhagen on the night train. She had bought me a necklace in Copenhagen Central Station. It had my favourite stone, amber. I thought it was a beautiful yellow. We had good time before we had to say goodbye. Mamma had tears in her eyes when she looked at me and told me to be careful, and wished me luck. We hugged and kissed goodbye.

I had taken the train destined for Hamburg. It took me through Denmark, to the small coastal city of Grossenbrode, and now I was on a train ferry to Bremerhaven, Germany, and from there I would go to Hamburg, where I would have to change trains. This was not the first time I had gone by myself to Germany, but I had always had family friends of my parents waiting for me, and I had never been to Munich. I was nineteen years old, and felt the whole world was mine.!

One day back in Stockholm, when school was near summer vacation, I got the brilliant idea to write to Klaus, an old boyfriend, who lived in Düsseldorf and was studying to be a doctor. I don't know if he knew anything about art, but I asked him if he knew of any art schools where I could study fashion. He replied quickly that there were fashion schools in Berlin, one in Düsseldorf, and one in Munich.

Pappa said I could not go to Berlin. I don't know why he got so huffy about it. I did not want to go to Düsseldorf. I've been there, and it's a beautiful city, but I did not want to be where Klaus was. So that left Munich, where I never had been, and neither had my parents. I applied to the school in Munich, and was accepted.

I had one year left at a commercial art school in Stockholm. I would not be an asset to anybody to draw a vacuum cleaner, or a barbecue, or even a scissor. Fashion was my thing. I thought maybe I would learnqw something new and more about fashion in a foreign school. I had grand plans of what I would do after school. I was going to work for one or two years in Germany, one or two years in America, and maybe work in England too. Then I would come home and I would be sure to get a job with all this experience!

Seagulls circulated the boat as the ferry came close to the shore. The wind had died down, with me looking like I had been through a hurricane. It was announced over the speaker system that everybody who came with the train was to go back to their seats on the train. The train was at the waterline. It smelled of seawater, and the cars were shaking back and forth, screeching as iron was hitting iron. The conductor unlocked all the cars, so now everybody was looking for their compartment.

I found my seat and had my passport stamped. Soon I was on my way to Hambur

CHAPTER 2

THE JOURNEY

I looked out the window and saw villages, houses, and cows sweeping by. Here on the coast the landscape was flat. The express train made only two stops. It was not very far to Hamburg, so I got my hair in order, put lipstick on, and I felt ready for Hamburg.

"Hamburg next," the conductor called. I gathered my new jacket and handbag. I had not been able to resist buying either, that last day in Stockholm. The handbag was very artsy, rough leather with big, thick, white ropes for the handle.

The train stopped with a jerk. My suitcase was a bit heavy and I dragged it down from the train steps. I found the train to Munich, it was also an express train, with only a few stops in between, but it was still a long way to Munich. I would be able to sleep a little on the train, hopefully.

It was very interesting to be standing there on that big central station platform. Not every locomotive was electric; most of them were coal or steam. There was a train that was heading for Italy. A couple of people took goats with them on the train! I don't know where the goats would be sitting. I heard this was not unusual for Italian people to bring farm animals with them on the train home. They, men usually, went to Germany to work, and when the work was finished for the season, they bought goats, and even hens and pigs, to take home to Italy. The animals were probably cheaper in Germany.

I could not stay and look any longer. I found my compartment, and put my heavy suitcase on the floor. Luckily, I didn't have to lift it. I settled in, with my ticket handy in my beautiful new purse. I took out a couple of Swedish magazines I had bought in Stockholm. It felt like it had been a long time since I left home with my mother and taken a cab down to central station. My dad had stood and waved goodbye.

The train jerked, and we slowly started rolling out of the station. The scenery was about the same as it was on the trip to Hamburg. I decided to read a little.

We stopped at Düsseldorf. I remembered the big Königs Alle, where designers like Gucci and Chanel had stores. I remembered the big trees in the middle of the street where people who wanted to be seen walked.

The next stop was Cologne, with its big, twin-spired Cologne Cathedral. Then we came to the beautiful Rhine River. I have nice memories of the Rhine. There is a little island in the middle of the river, where only a tower fits. Called Mouse Tower, it was built around the year 968, and the story goes that a mean king was eaten alive there by mice. Another legend also tells of beautiful women who sat on the rocks there, and waved to the seamen to come. When the men came, they cut the boats on the sharp cliffs, and drowned.

On both sides of the river are mountains and hills blue with grapes for the Rhine wine that makes the Rhine so famous. By the edge of the river is a little town called Rüdesheim. I have been there a few times; it's so pretty, and you can take the ferry across the river to Bingen. Bingen is also nice, but that is where the US army station is located. The beer garden is full of US soldiers.

We did not stop in Rüdesheim now, but only went along the river for a while. Frankfurt, another stop. I knew that you could fly direct to Frankfurt. Some of the flights from Stockholm to Germany go to Hamburg first. There you had to get off the plane, go into the flight hall, go through customs, and then go back to your airplane. That was always so much work. It is better to go by train.

At last the conductor announced, "Munich, next stop!" My heart jumped. This was it! Here my life would change, but I just didn't know it.

CHAPTER 3

MUNICH

I looked out the window, searching for Walter, a friend of my parents' who was to pick me up. He better have not forgotten that I was coming! But there he was; it took a second before he saw me. He had not changed a bit; he still reminded me of Bugs Bunny!

Walter saw me, and came running. He asked for my suitcase, and I happily let him carry it off the train.

The central station was big. Sounds of trains coming and going and music playing over speakers echoed. There were smells from restaurants, perfume stores, pizza places; everything was there. Walter asked if I was hungry. I was almost too excited to eat, so I had only a wurst. Munich is known for their wursts, meaning all kinds of hotdogs and sausages.

We finally made it out to the street and the car, a small Volkswagen Beetle. Walter with his long legs, why did he choose such a small car? We packed my suitcase and my handbag into the car. That's when he broke the news that he had not looked in the paper for a room for me. Suddenly I did not feel too well. He said, convincingly, that he had today's newspaper, and we would look in the paper together. Okay, I said, what else could I do?

It turned out to be not as easy as he had thought. There was nothing in the city, "not where respectful people live," he said. He finally found something outside of Munich, and I would have to go by train into the city for school. Train? I got a little bit irritated with "Bugs Bunny," but then again, there was nothing I could do. Walter called the people that rented out the room. It was still for rent, and the person that answered gave him the address and told him how to get there.

Walter drove to show me how to get to my school from the rail station. It was not far, about a fifteen- or twenty-minute walk from the station. Straight up the street from the station was a big fountain with people sitting on the edges. From there we took a right, onto a street called Sonnenblum Strasse. Then straight on Sonnenblum Strasse to a street with the name Am Rossmarkt 1. There was my school building, the first one on that street, with a great big wooden door. The whole thing looked very old to me. Walter told me that the school had been a nunnery over a hundred of years ago. I thought it was very interesting. On Monday, I would start school. I would meet new people. I wondered what the classrooms would look like.

Now we headed out to "my room," wherever that was. It was on a small street, with pretty houses, and every house had a small fence around the garden. The gardens were full of fruit trees, bushes, and flowers. It was a nice area. I guess that's what Walter meant when he said "respectful people" lived here!

We stopped at a house and got out of the car. We rang the bell that was on the locked gate. A woman's voice come on the speaker: "Who is it?" Walter said who we were. The gate buzzed and Walter opened it, and let me in first. It was a few steps to the front door, and a woman wearing an apron came out. She was baking, she told us. The woman, Frau Müller was her name, showed us the room. It was the first room to the right, after the bathroom. Walter went to the car and brought in my suitcase and my other belongings. After that he had to leave, but first we made a plan that he was going to pick me up in the evening, and go to a jazz club he knew.

Frau Müller asked where I was from, how long I planned to stay, what I was doing, and whether I wanted the room with breakfast. She would wake me in the mornings, then come with the breakfast before I left for school for the day. She told me which train to take, and where the train station was, just a five-minute walk away through the backyard.

She told me that this room had been her daughter's, but that they needed money for a reason that I cannot remember if she told me. The daughter had given them her room to rent out, as economic help. They also had a son, I think he was eighteen years old, and the daughter was twenty. There was also a Herr Müller.

The room was pretty, light, and feminine. It was furnished with a makeup table with a round mirror and a ruffled skirt. The room also had a sink, to wash your face and brush your teeth, with a drape around it, for privacy I guess. Outside the window was an apple tree. It was all very pretty. Frau Müller said after eight o'clock in the evenings, I could take a bath or a shower. Then she left, and I sank down on the bed. I was tired, and I just wanted to lie down and sleep.

I woke up and looked at my watch. It was 7:35 p.m.! I was up like shot out of a canon! Walter should be here in twenty-five minutes! What was I going to wear? I opened my suitcase, hoping to find something that wouldn't need ironing. I got a hold of a green sleeve, pulled it out, and my grass-green dress appeared. Yes, that will do. It was one my mother had sewn. I found my beige high heel shoes, put my hair up, put on lipstick and mascara; finished! The doorbell rang just as I was putting on my last shoe. I got the house key so I would not wake the Müllers if I came back late.

I didn't know where we were, only that the club was in Munich. Walter bought us tickets at the door, and a beer when we were inside. I don't like beer, and one was enough for me for the whole night. It was so smoky that you could cut it, and I did not have to speak, because nobody would have been able to hear me anyway. The music was good; I like jazz, it's one of my favourites.

That was my first night in Munich. And honestly, I would rather have stayed home and slept!

CHAPTER 4

GERMAN MASTER SCHOOL OF FASHION

Sunday came and went. I went for a walk in the neighbourhood, just to get to know the area, and to find out where the railroad station was. I was glad it was not far to the station, but there were not many stores there. An ice cream bar and a magazine and newspaper stand, that was it. My station was Aubing South. It is always good to know the name of the station, your address, and where you are going to get off the train.

The few people I met said politely, *"Grüss Gott,"* that is the greeting when you meet somebody in Bavaria. The same as our "Hello," only, I thought, a bit nicer. Also, many seemed to go to church. Here in Bavaria, most of the people are Catholic, and every village had two churches, one Catholic and one Lutheran Protestant.

I had not had breakfast, so I went into the ice cream bar. I saw they were also serving coffee and cake, so I had Italian cake, and it was delicious. Most of the ice cream bars here are Italian.

When I returned to my room, I was still tired from everything, so I lay down on my bed and slept. I was awakened by a knock at the door; it was Frau Müller. She had seen me come in earlier, and she offered me a plate of goulash. They had had that for dinner, and there was a lot left. I was hungry, and I happily accepted.

Monday morning came quickly. School started at nine o'clock, but first I had to register as a new student, and of course I had to go to school by train. This was all new for me, but somehow nice too. The train ride took about twenty minutes. I stood still for a second at the big Munich central station and looked around. I was amazed and astonished that I, Birgit, was standing here in Munich, all by myself, not knowing a soul.

I looked up Bahnhof Strasse. I was going to go all the way to the big fountain, and then turn right. I had better start walking. People were quickly going by me, stores where opening, things were being delivered. The sun was shining, and I walked along the street, smiling. I was happy and free, and I could do what I wanted. I felt so lucky!

I sped up, but in the middle of traffic noise, I thought I heard horse hooves on the pavement. I looked over my shoulder and saw the prettiest big horse pulling a wagon! The horse had lots of hair around its hooves, and it was big and wide, with lots of hair. It was beautiful. It stopped outside a store I had just walked past. He delivered milk! A man, the coachman, had on a big long leather apron. Oh, it was like a painting from a time long ago. The coachman took a big block of ice from the wagon with a big tong, and carried the ice into the store. I wanted to stay and watch longer, but I had to leave if I wanted to be at school on time.

I came to Rossmarkt 1, and the big wooden door was wide open. This was *Deutsche Meisterschule für Mode* (German Masterschool for Fashion), as a sign with gold letters proudly stated. Some students arrived, and I asked them where I would find the office.

At the office, I went through all the formalities, filled in all the papers, and got my picture taken for my student pass and for my pass for the train and streetcars. Soon I was on the way to my classroom, two floors up.

CHAPTER 5

SECOND FLOOR

The stairs to the second floor ascended in a spiral. Dark grey, with shells still imprinted in them, the stone stairs were deeply worn from thousands of footsteps over the years.

The classroom door was closed. I knocked, and looked in. Students were spread all over the floor; there didn't seem to be any order to the classroom. The teacher approached me and asked if I was Miss Andersson. I said yes. She presented me to the class, and told them that I was from Sweden.

Sweden was not very popular these days after Ulla Jacobsson appeared in the movie, *One Summer of Happiness*, and Anita Ekberg appeared in *La Dolce Vita*. And by the looks on the students' faces, I was not either.

The teacher had draped a big piece of material over a chair, and we were told to draw it. I started, but I was not sure how to draw a wide piece of black-and-white striped material. The teacher wanted it exact. It took me the whole day, and everybody's work looked the same. I thought it would have to get better tomorrow.

After school, I walked slowly to the train station. I was in no hurry, because I had two hours before the train left. There was a fruit stand on my way, so I stopped and bought a half pound of cherries in a paper cone. They were dark red and tasted good. I held my new handbag tightly; it was now filled with pens and markers and all the things that I needed for drawing.

I looked into store windows and a couple of cafes. Had I not passed a bookstore on the way to school? Yes, there it was. Excited, I went in. It was big and had every type of paper! My kind of store. I needed drawing paper, and here they had the cheapest type of paper, I think it was a kind of recycled newspaper, sold by the sheet for ten cents a sheet. It was nice, kind of brownish-red. I had noticed they did a lot of kohl drawing at the school. I had never liked kohl; I draw with India ink, and that might be interesting on this loose paper. I also looked for a nice book to read, and found one on art history. I bought the book, along with nice writing paper and cards, so I would need to find a post office for stamps, but not today.

When I got to the train station, I asked where to find the train to Aubing South. The ticket seller answered, but I did not understand him, he spoke Bavarian. But I thanked him anyway, and went to ask someone else. Finally, I found my train; it was already in. I sank into my seat and almost fell asleep. It had been a long and adventurous day.

Back in my room, I unpacked my bags, happy about my purchases. At eight o'clock, I had a shower, then picked out my clothes for tomorrow. After I wrote a short letter to my parents, I rolled over and slept.

CHAPTER 6

SCHOOL DAYS

Every day, I met my favourite horse delivering the milk! I loved the horse, and wondered what its name was. I would have liked to stand there and look at it for a minute, but I always had to rush to school. As I went through the big wooden portal and directly up the stairs, I always thought about all the nuns who had gone up and down those stairs, perhaps while praying.

One day we drew portraits. I had never done that before, and the teacher chose me to sit as the model. She informed the students that they should be aware that everything about Miss Andersson was round. I did not want to be round! But the teacher went on, saying the students should notice the eyes and the mouth and the form of the face. I did not want to know any more. I never saw the outcome of my modelling, and I don't think I really wanted to.

Usually, one day went by just like the other, but one day we went to the zoo. The teacher just decided, right on the spot, that we were going to the zoo because it was such nice weather. We were told to take pens and paper along, and were going to spend the day out there and draw. I think the streetcar went there, but one of the male students offered me a ride in his car, which made me even less popular. He drove me, but then we separated at the zoo, and

I walked by myself and explored. There was a green.parrot, and it was old, I had been told. As soon as I stood beside him, he flexed his wing and said, "Hail Hitler!" That parrot was a celebrity at the zoo!

I walked around, and it was nice to see all the animals. I came to what I thought of as my favourite, flamingos. Not that they had always been my favourite birds ever, but they stood still. You could come back in an hour, and they had not moved a feather. I just can't draw animals that move the whole time. Animals are hard to draw, anyway. But this was very nice. I could stand there and draw forever.

Every day, on my way home, I walk by a car repair shop where guys were working outside on the cars. This time as I was passing the shop, a young guy my age came to me and said, "*Grüss Gott*, I see you walking by every day, and I wonder if I could invite you for a movie. Maybe tonight, if you have time?" I didn't have anything else to do, so why not have a bit of company, I thought. I agreed, told him where I lived, and because it was a small town, he knew the people; he had fixed their car one time.

His name was Dieter, and he picked me up by eight-thirty, as he said he would. His car was an old DKW. I don't know how old, but very old, if you ask me. The drive was not very comfortable, especially when we came to a small ditch. I was very concerned where it all was going to end up. It was not the way to the movie, that's for sure. Dieter just took off through the high grass that the farmers cut for the cows. Then he stopped the car and got out. He picked up a can of gas from the high grass. He told me that he fills up the can at work, and hides it here. Free gas! Dieter suddenly lost his charm, and was not as nice-looking as I first thought.

The school days went by, and I liked it, but I didn't love it. I loved the way to and from school, especially going to the station. I always checked out the art stores, there was a big one on my route to school, but I could not buy much, because I didn't have much money. I just bought my cherries. And I always looked for a skull! Of everything I wanted to buy, it was a skull I wanted most. I had it in my head that you were a good artist if you had a skull sitting in your room. I think I had been in the sun too much! I found one though, and I looked at it every day.

CHAPTER 7

SATURDAY

The days went by, and it was always same thing, with nothing special going on in school. I woke up every day at the same time, had the same breakfast, got dressed, collected my papers, pencils, and water colours, and off I went. The street was quiet today and the train was emptier than usual. I wondered if it was a holiday or something. I made my way to school, which by now had become a routine. I turned the corner at Rossmarkt, and arrived at my school. The big wooden door was closed. I banged on the door. A small square window opened, and a face looked out. I said, "*Grüss Gott*, my name is Birgit Andersson, and I'm a student here."

The face said, "The school opens on Monday. You young people are funny; when there's no school you show up, and when there is school you don't come. It's Saturday today!"

I felt stupid. I didn't know what to do. I sat down by the fountain. It was a little bit moist, but it was nice in the sun with the splashing water and the soft wind that carried the water droplets like an angel's shower over me. I sat still for a moment, listening to the noises around me. Somebody had a radio playing music. I had a little white and gold transistor radio that I got from Pappa before I left. I had always music on, day or night. Now I started reading. I had a book on how to learn Greek that I carried with me all the time, in case I would have time to learn.

As I sat and read, I felt somebody looking at me. I looked up and saw a blond, suntanned man. He was full of compliments, and he asked me where I was from. I told him I was from Sweden, and he laughed. He was from Finland, and spoke Swedish. His name was Raimo; he was a sculptor and had won a prize as the best young sculptor in Finland that year. His prize was a trip to visit all the big art exhibitions in Europe. He would go to Paris, Rome, Venice, and, of course, Greece. He had showed me a picture of the statue for which he had won the prize. It was a modern, heavy stone sculpture of a woman. He was thirty-one, and had been married. He lived in Helsinki. There was another man with him, and he introduced him as his friend Sten, a director of documentary films.

Raimo's eyes were fixed on me, and he asked if he could do anything for me. I said no, I was on my way home. Then he asked if he could invite me for dinner. Yes, that he could, and the three of us went to a nearby restaurant. I don't remember, but I most likely had goulash again; I love goulash! To drink, I always had apple juice. Raimo stared at me the whole time, and when it was time to say goodbye, I had to promise that I would come to the railway station tomorrow, before they would go by bus to Paris. He wanted me to go with him, but that was a definite no.

It was Sunday, and everybody was dressed in their Sunday best. So was I. I had on a white skirt and a blue-and-white striped top, white shoes with a little bit of a heel, and carried my favourite purse. Everybody was going to church, but I was going to Munich by train, to say goodbye to a guy that I had just met yesterday.

There they stood, beside the bus. Raimo held a red rose. He gave me the rose and kissed me on the cheek. I felt like a teenager! We had time for a coffee before they were called to the bus. We exchanged addresses, and I gave him both my home address in Stockholm and my address in Munich. He gave me his address in

Helsinki. We exchanged a hug and a promise to write, and I wished him a great journey.

I went directly home on the train; I was exhausted. I saw that the Müllers were home from church, and were sitting in the garden. But I went into my room and lay down on my bed. I did not even have time to think; I could do that later.

I heard a knock on my door. It was Monica, the Müllers' daughter, whose room I was renting. This was the first time I had met her. She came in, sat on a chair, and told me a group of young people from their church were getting together at a friend's place. She was wondering if I wanted to join them. It was just three houses down the street, and we would go together at around eight o'clock. I said yes, but I said I was not Catholic. She said it did not matter.

I was not sure about this Catholic business. I had no idea if they were going to sit and pray, or what they would be doing at this youth meeting. I only knew one person who was Catholic, a girl I had gone to grammar school with. She was not in class when we had religion. There was one Catholic church that I knew of in Stockholm, and that was by the big library.

The evening was warm. When we arrived, there were people sitting outside. There were some chairs, but you could also sit on the grass; I sat down on the grass. They told me their names. There was no Miss or Mister, just first names. Everyone was about my age.

They spoke Bavarian, and I had a hard time following. They didn't pray, but the host went into their parents' house, and came out with bottles wine. The parents were gone for the night, and they wouldn't notice a couple of missing bottles of wine. It was more than a couple, but it didn't matter to me; I didn't drink wine, apple juice was good enough for me.

I found the meeting—or party—interesting. I had thought that people who were Catholic were deeply religious, way more than we Lutherans. And here they were, drinking and talking, borrowing wine from their parents' wine cellar. I guess "borrowing" wasn't the right word.

CHAPTER 8

MEETING URBAN

One day after school, I went to the ice cream bar for a banana split. After all, I could not live on cherries alone! I sat down and ordered, then noticed a guy sitting near me. He ordered an iced coffee. Beside him were drawings and a small portfolio. Oh, I thought, an artist. When we got our orders, he kept looking at me. I stood up to go to my train.

The train was empty, and I was the only one in the compartment until I heard somebody come in. I looked up, and there was the guy from the ice cream bar. We both smiled, and said *Grüss Gott*. He said that he had to go and catch another train, and asked if we could meet tomorrow at the same place after school. He went to the Academy of Fine Arts. I agreed to meet him after school. I had gotten a glimpse of the drawing that he carried, and it was a very nice portrait of a man. I thought I could probably learn something from this guy, so I was glad that we were going to meet again. I found it surprising that at school we had to draw like the teacher did. I did not like that; it destroyed the style I had when I started there. And I was good, I had been the second-best in fashion classes at home, and now I just did not know how to draw!

The next day after school, I went to meet my date. I had not a clue what his name was. I saw him as soon as I turned the corner, inside the station. He saw me, and came up to me, smiling. We said *Grüss Gott*, and then we introduced ourselves. His name was Urban.

Now that we got that cleared up, what were we going to do? Urban thought we could take the streetcar to Schwabing. It was a part of the city where artists live and hang out. He said there was a club there where we could get something to eat and listen to jazz music.

So, we took the streetcar to Schwabing. There was one club after the other, and we found the club we were looking for. A lot of smoke met us when we opened the door. It was early and the club seemed to be full of locals. Do these people not work, I thought? We found a table, and ordered potato soup with a wiener wurst.

CHAPTER 9

THE PARTY

My days were no longer like they once were. Urban would be sitting on a bench outside the school every day, waiting for me to get out. We would meet up with his friends, and figure out what to do. Usually it was going to a bar, with music and dancing. But today they said we were going to go to Urban's house and wait there for some other people to join us. A girlfriend of theirs was going to have a party at her home.

We drove to Urban's house. I was all eyes as we drove through the Bavarian landscape, noticing beautiful old farmhouses and lots of cows (my favourite).The guys were talking the whole time, but I was not really listening; I was in my own world. In the middle of a road that seemed to go directly up to heaven, the car stopped, and Urban stepped out and opened a big, heavy gate, to let us in with the car. What is this place, I thought? There was a barn on the left side, but in front of us, and where all of us went in, was a little side door to a big atelier, with windows from floor to ceiling on the whole long wall. Inside there were sofas, big chairs, a sofa table, a bed, and a heater for wood or coal. There were cow hides on the floor. It was Urban's room.

The other friends had obviously been there many times before, and they put on an Elvis record and opened soft drinks that stood in a box in a corner. Finally, the other guys showed up, and we could start thinking of partying. We all went outside and piled into the big Mercedes. We made a U-turn, and went out the open gate. It was crowded in the car, and we were singing. We headed for the party.

The trip was not that long, only about half an hour. We scrambled out of the car; you were out of luck if you were wearing a skirt, it got all wrinkled up. But who would notice in that crowd? The girl that was hosting the party was pretty and nice, and she welcomed us in, and soon we were mingling with the rest of the guests. There were many people, but it was a big house, actually the biggest house I had ever been in. I wondered what her parents did for a living. I later learned that he was a general. The kids told me that he was, or had been, a Nazi.

The party went on late into the night. It was fun; they were all intellectual kids and there was a lot of talking, but there was a lot of dancing, too. Interestingly enough, there was not that much alcohol like there would have been in Sweden at such a big party, where everybody could be drinking whatever they wanted and as much as they liked. I thought this was really great.

CHAPTER 10

END OF TERM

The school term would soon be ending. In Germany there is only one month of summer vacation. I had two weeks extra in Munich before I was going home. Before the first weekend, Urban come to me and said that his mother wanted to see me, and that I was invited to spend the weekend there. I was not sure that I liked that idea,

Urban said I would stay in a guesthouse above a restaurant. What did they mean? I was not impressed, I did not want to be that familiar. But I said okay, and politely thanked him for the invitation.

Saturday came quickly. I packed an overnight bag, and Urban came to pick me up. We went to the train station together, and we had to change trains in Munich. I was far from excited, but the views were spectacular. There were mountains, it was a whole change in the scenery. The train stopped at every milk stand, it seemed.

Finally, I thought we were there, but no, we had to take a bus. But it was not bad; I actually enjoyed it. The towns the bus stopped in were so pretty with Bavarian houses, pubs, and women with baskets they used for shopping.

The bus took us on a winding road through woods that were nice and clean, and I could see far between the trees. There were signs to watch out for frogs. Frogs crossed over the street, Urban told me, and there were people who took care of the frogs. There were also signs to watch out for deer. It was a beautiful forest, almost like a picture in a storybook. I almost expected to see a bunny hiding behind a tree, or a troll looking stunned by the bus! Suddenly the woods ended, and we were in the village where Urban lived. It was amazingly beautiful, like stepping back in time.

We walked a little way through the high grass. Cows were on one side, and a house with all kinds of feathered animals was on the other side. And in front was a typical farmhouse, the bottom half white and the upper half wood. It had white shutters with a heart in the middle on all the windows. It was the backside of my "hotel." There was parking space and a meat store and a stall, I guess for the cows. There was gravel in front of the hotel, which was mainly a pub and restaurant all in one.

My room was typical old Bavarian style. I liked it, and thought it was nice. The down duvet on the bed was so high that you could not see anything else. The window was facing the way we had just come. Through the field was the bus station, and there was also a train station. The train did not run that often, so bus was more convenient.

We then went downstairs to the restaurant and had dinner. Urban went home, then came back and told me that his mother wanted to see me at two o'clock the next day. I had thought it was strange that Urban had not brought me directly to his home to say hello. Maybe it was the custom here, I don't know.

I slept very well, and when I woke, I looked over the duvet to see it was not even seven o'clock, and I thought I might sleep a little bit longer. Just as I thought that, a terrible scream came from downstairs.

I ran to the window and looked out. Oh my God, it was a pig they had killed! My heart nearly stopped. Just under the guest room window they had killed a pig! And at this time in the morning! Maybe they wanted me up, so they could vacuum the room? No, but surely the cutlets would be fresh!

I might as well get up, and get cleaned up and dressed before Urban comes, I thought. Just as I came downstairs, Urban arrived. He showed me to a table, and we sat down and had our breakfast of coffee and buns, butter, and marmalade, the usual breakfast they had there.

CHAPTER 11

STAIRS

Urban was going to show me a bit of his town, which was very cute from what I had already seen. We walked out into the early morning sun to the town square. It was a little plain, with grass in the middle, and there was a maypole! It was blue and white, the Bavarian colours, and through it ran the main street.

Urban took my hand and led me through the middle.

There was a small path with gravel in the middle, the rest worn by many years of people stepping on the grass. It was a path, Urban told me, that all the farmers used when they were going to the church that was on top of the hill. This path was very old, it was there before the street was made.

On one side were a few old farmhouses, and on the other side was a big, slanting, grassy field with cows. There was another fence with goats. Goat cheese, was my first thought! The view was very beautiful; I could see church towers miles away, and mountaintops in the background. A soft wind carried the smell of roses from the gardens of the old farmhouses the other side of the path.

There were only four houses, and they had each a big flowering garden and fruit trees. The second house was Urban's mother's. There was a gravel path to the house with roses on both sides. The fruit trees were in bloom, and there were flowering bushes and a white picket fence with a gate. The whole thing looked like a beautiful painting.

Not far from Mother's little gate was a bench for anybody to sit and rest. We sat down for a while and looked at the grand view, then we started up the steep hill. We passed the other two farmhouses, and came to the forest edge, and the little path smelled fresh, full of pine needles and sap. There were stairs made of sticks that had been pressed into the ground. The stairs stopped after a few, and there was a wooden post with a carved wood picture of Jesus walking with the cross, in his pain and suffering. The stairs started again, and we climbed another few steps to another carved wood picture of Jesus. We kept climbing, and altogether there were ten woodcarvings on the way up, the last carving with Jesus on the cross.

I cannot imagine how the old ladies and old man could walk all these stairs, almost up to heaven, even though there was a bench halfway up where they could rest. As a young person, I could hardly take another step!

And there, on the top of the hill, was a beautiful old church. But there were more stairs! They were part of the church, but there were not many, and they were wide. At the bottom of the stairs, on either side, stood an angel, looking very peaceful. Looking as if she was saying something to you.

I should have listened.

Then there was a castle. Urban wanted me to see the inside of the castle and to see the view from the top, he said the scenery was fantastic. There was no elevators and he wanted me to walk all the way up. I said no thank you, I was tired of stairs. Instead, we walked in the courtyard, it was a high-fenced-in area around the castle. Urban said hello to almost everyone, and proudly introduced me as his Swedish girlfriend. The people said something in a Bavarian dialect that I didn't understand. I hoped that Urban's mother would speak real German. I asked Urban if we should maybe start going toward his mother's house.

CHAPTER 12

MEETING URBAN'S MOTHER

This time we walked on the street opposite of the old church path. But it still was not easy! The road was so steep, I felt like I should lean backward. A deep ditch was on one side, and on the other side was a steep hill. Urban held my hand the whole way because it was easy to slide on the loose gravel.

A grocery store was immediately in the curve facing us. Then the road turned sharply to the right. Was that not asking for accidents, I wondered aloud? Urban told me there had been a gruesome accident a couple of years ago in the winter. Two horses pulling a load of wood came in at a gallop, and could not stop. They ran right through the store windows and into the store. They went all the way to the other end of the store. The horses were all cut up and there was blood everywhere. I don't remember what Urban said had happened to the people in the store; hearing about the horses was enough for me!

"And here we are," Urban said, as we stood at the gate. Urban opened the gate, and like children we skipped down the driveway. Urban led me to the front of the house, facing the old church way.

"Can you wait here?" Urban asked. "I'll see if Mother is ready." I nodded as I wondered what I had gotten myself into.

Urban showed up in the doorway, took me by the arm, and said, "My mother will see you for tea in her sitting room. It's upstairs; I will go with you and show you."

It was dark, and an old staircase with a long, handwoven rug, led upstairs. The ceiling was low; I guess it was probably to keep the heat in the house better. Upstairs was a big hallway leading out to a balcony, and on the left was a door. Urban knocked on the door and a woman's voice said, "Come in."

Urban's mother was sitting on a rococo sofa. She held out her hand over the table, and as I took her hand she smiled and said, "Everybody calls me 'Mother.' You can call me Mother, too."

I did not want to call her Mother; she was not my mother, I thought, and got a bit huffy.

"And your name is Brigitte?" she asked.

"No, Birgit," I corrected. She nodded to Urban to go out. He left and closed the door. I was alone with Urban's mother. She asked me to sit down, so I sat, and thanked her for the invitation.

I looked around. The windows were small, as they were in old times. There was a white cowhide on the floor. The room was sparsely furnished, and most of the furniture was Jugendstil.

Mother smiled at me in a friendly way, and she asked what my plans were when I finished school. I told her that I had another year at art school, and then I planned to find work as a commercial artist. Then she asked what my mother did; if she worked. I told her my mother was working, and at what. She then asked what my father was he working with. I did not like the questions; they rubbed me the wrong way.

The tea was good, and there were cookies on a silver plate. Our conversation was a bit lopsided, as I did not say much. Instead, I took notice of the starched white tablecloth, the thin chinaware, and the silver sugar bowl and creamer. The most impressive thing in the room was a big, hammered silver bowl with her knitting yarn. It was just beautiful!

A knock at the door interrupted us, and in came a girl somewhat my age.

"Mother, Uncle Max would like to talk to Birgit," she said.

The girl told me on the way down the stairs that she was Urban's older sister, Sabine. "Nice to meet you," she said, as she opened an old door with an equally old door handle.

The door closed behind me, and there in the middle of the room stood a tall, skinny man, about my father's age. He was a man, from what I have heard, for whom everybody had respect. He was Max von Schlosshof, the judge from Munich.

CHAPTER 13

MEETING MAX VON SCHLOSSHOF

Mr. von Schlosshof had a stern look on his face as he looked me over.

I said, "Hello, my name is Birgit."

"Hello Birgit, Urban has told me a lot about you; it is nice to meet you. Have a seat." He pointed to a chair.

"Call me Uncle Max, as all the others do," he said with a little bit of a smile, which took the edge off my nervousness.

Uncle Max was of thin build, and was not as tall as Mother. He had an aquiline nose, and looked very aristocratic, which I knew he was. I looked around the room, and saw a shiny black grand piano. On it was a vase filled with a big bunch of pink peonies. This was apparently also where the family ate, as there was a big table and a corner bench.

Uncle Max asked me so many questions, it was like a cross examination. What were my plans? Who were my parents and what did they do? And when he was finished with questions about my parents, it was my grandparents' turn.

My grandparents were in north Sweden, I told him, my grandmother wove rugs and tablecloths, and my grandfather worked in the forest, taking down trees. I had not a clue what they called it, if anything. I was sweating, because I didn't know how to say all of this in German. God help me, I thought.

Uncle Max was not finished. What did my other grandparents in Stockholm do? Did I have any sisters or brothers? No, I did not. By that point, it was the only thing I was sure of!

I looked over at the grand piano and Uncle Max said, "It's Mother who plays. She sings opera and Schubert Lieder. She used to sing a lot, but now she is working in the pharmacy, which does not leave much time over for what she really loves, which is music. She will sing for you."

Finally, the questioning was over. I went out into the afternoon sun. Urban was sitting and waiting for me. He hugged me and asked, "How did it go?" Did you survive?"

"That wasn't easy!" I said. I felt really tired. "I'll go back to the hotel and lie down for a while. Uncle Max said he wants to invite everybody for chicken dinner at the restaurant. See what time he says, and I will meet you downstairs then. I am really tired."

CHAPTER 14

DINNER WITH THE FAMILY

I woke with a start when I heard a knock at my door. Urban stood there. He gave me a kiss and asked, "Are you ready?"

I said. "No, do I look like it?"

I found my shoes in my bag, under the clothes I had with me. They were pretty—blue and white, with a sling back and a high heel. A look of approval from Urban, and I closed the door behind me.

Urban's family was already seated. I met Urban's youngest sister, Ullie. We shook hands. She was very pretty with thick dark hair, in contrast to Urban and Sabine, who were so blond, like almost white. Urban told me, that there were two years' age difference between all the kids. So Urban was one year older than me, and Ullie was one year younger than me.

I sat next to Ullie, and Urban sat right across from us. Dinner was a whole chicken and *Brötchen*, or pretzels. Everybody had wine with their meal.

Ullie was very nice and funny. I instantly liked her. She said she was only home for a couple of days. She was studying chemistry and biology at the University of Frankfurt, and she had only one term more to go. When she was finished university, her job was going to be to check the drinking water in public buildings.

"When I am finished university," she told me, "I am not coming back to Munich. Mother wants me here, but I am going to stay in Frankfurt."

My response was a curious, "Oh?"

Ullie went on, "Mother thinks she can tell me what to do and when to do it, at all times. It's easier when you live farther away."

Sabine told me she was working as a bank teller, close to the central station in Munich, and went to work every morning by train. Uncle Max also went by train to Munich every morning. He worked in the Justice Building. I thought he would at least drive a Mercedes. But no car for Uncle Max. Mother drove a two-seater Karmann Giah!

Mother and Uncle Max also joined in the conversation. We had a great time, eating and drinking, and afterward we had coffee. I thanked them very much for the dinner and nice evening.

Urban went up with me, and we made plans for the next day. Urban thought we should take the bus to Ammersee and go sailing. I told him I had never sailed, but he said that didn't matter, that he had been sailing many times, so I agreed to go.

The bus ride there was nice, and as always, the houses were beautiful. Their balconies and windows all had tons of flowers. In the background we could see the Alps.

The fresh breeze from the sea hit us when we got off the bus. The water was a glittering blue, and there were many white sails out already. It smelled of water, tar, and fish, all at once. The sun was beautiful, and we didn't want to waste any time, so we went directly to the guy that rents out the boats.

To our disappointment, all the small sailboats were already rented. The only sailboat he had was a big one that would require more than two people to sail. Urban somehow convinced him that we could handle the big boat, so we got it.

Urban set sail. He gave me some ropes to hang on to, and he took the rudder. It was nice, the water was splashing up on us, and we were in the middle of the lake. I could see some small clouds when a horn suddenly sounded. That meant every boat had to go to shore, because a storm was coming.

The lake lay deep, meaning that on all sides were high mountains. It suddenly turned dark, and the storm threw itself on the lake. Most of the sailboats were in, then all of them were, except for us. The wind was coming in with a vengeance. The waves were getting higher. I was scared, and my only hope was that Urban could maneuver the boat to shore, but the rudder was not even in the water anymore. I braced my heels on the edge of the boat, holding onto that rope. I was wet. The sea was roaring, and the blue water had turned black. Suddenly I was hanging outside the boat, which had pitched on its side. Urban screamed into the wind, "If we fall, throw yourself backward so you don't come into the sails! Otherwise you might drown!"

The storm was over, as suddenly as it had come. During the storm, the rental guy had been looking for us through binoculars, the two kids in the big boat. We had another hour on our boat rental—no thank you. I could hardly walk, never mind my swollen hands.

That was my first time sailing, which also turned out to be my last.

CHAPTER 15

LETTER FROM HOME

My cousin Kjell, the son of my mother's sister in north Sweden, would be having his fifteenth birthday in a few days. I used to spend summer vacations with him and his family. When I was fifteen years old, I was living with them for the summer, and during my first week there I had a motorcycle accident. They thought I was going to die. It had been the first of July, exactly five years ago.

Even though I had been thinking about Kjell's birthday the whole time, I still forgot it. On the date of his birthday, I remembered it, and went out and bought a "Sorry I'm late" card. Very funny, I thought, and mailed it right away.

A few days later, I had a letter from home. I opened the letter from my mother, and started reading. Suddenly I stopped. I could not believe what I was reading! I felt my throat tighten up. My card had arrived same day as Kjell's funeral. Kjell had been driving a moped that he had borrowed from his grandpa, and had been hit by a car and instantly died. That was on the third of July.

The next day, Urban and I went to a big church and lit a candle for Kjell, and sat down in deep thoughts.

CHAPTER 16

URBAN'S SCHOOL

By now, I have been seeing Urban every single day since we met in the ice cream bar. Today he wanted to show me where he had gotten his education in woodworking.

Urban told me that he had received his education in professional trades from the Franciscan Order in the Buchoof monastery right after the war. He had learned carpentry and furniture making. He attended for four years in all, including apprenticeships, then got his diploma.

I was on my way to meet my first monks. I wondered what I should wear. I did not have that much to choose from, but I had a dress I had not worn yet. Mamma had sewn it for me, and it was the prettiest material, it looked like it was hand painted, with flowers in a field. The dress had short sleeves, a high neckline in front, and the back was cut out in a deep scoop. That's the one I would wear, with white shoes.

This school was not far from the railway station, so we walked there. We came to a long iron fence with a gate. The gate was open, but the path to the schoolhouse itself was closed off. It was vacation time for them, too.

The only path open was to the church. Urban said it was open day and night, so we walked in. The church was not very big, but nevertheless, it was nice. We lit a candle, and silently walked around to find a place to sit down. There were a few people spread out in the pews. Some sat with their head bent in prayer; some looked up.

A woman passed us. She turned around behind me, and made the sign of a cross. What had made her upset? I, in turn upset, asked Urban. He answered, "Your bare back." So much for my pretty dress that I can only wear in Sweden, I thought!

But I was really amazed by Urban's ability to recite all the prayers in Latin along with the priest. Urban is Lutheran, not Catholic, but he knew a lot about the Catholic religion. He said they had to learn it in school, and it was a hard regimen. They prayed all kinds of different prayers at different times, and all in Latin.

So there we stood, outside the gate again. And I had not seen any monks! I guess they would have looked like any other man on the street.

CHAPTER 17

A VISITOR

I had hardly sat down when I heard the sounds of the doorbell. It was never for me, unless Urban visited, and he had just left after our visit to his school. It was Mother, and I could not have been more surprised if the president of the United States would have walked in!

I offered her a seat on the sofa. She sat down and said, "Birgit, you are coming to live with us. It is not good for a young woman to live alone and have a man as a guest. I'm talking about Urban. It wouldn't be good for the Judge of Munich's reputation if that should come out. We have a big house, and we want you live with us while you are in Munich. I will write to your mother, and I think she will agree."

What does she mean? Does it not look funny when a girl moves in with a boy? I was stunned, and I didn't know what to say. Had I not been so well behaved and polite, I would have said what I thought. And this is one of my big regrets. I did not see what was happening. The first thread of the web had been woven.

CHAPTER 18

URBAN'S HOME

I had kicked off my shoes. The grass between my toes was soft, and it felt and smelled so nice. Small bees and even a bumble bee were humming beside me. It was a warm summer day in this sunny field, full of buttercups, forget-me-nots, and clover. Actually, it was on the hill of a dirt road. I liked to sit here in the grass among all these small flowers and see how many I recognized.

I did not want to think about yesterday, when Mother so suddenly got me to move to her and Urban's house. I still don't understand why I was here. I did not want to get this close with Urban, or his family.

But here I was, sitting in the warm grass with my paint box, searching for my sunglasses that I had dropped in the grass someplace. I actually liked sitting here and listening to the sounds of nature at my feet, and to a machine saw across the road.

I was waiting for Urban. He had wanted me to go with him, and see where he worked. He was working with an old man in an old woodworking shop. I don't know what they were making, probably a cabinet. I liked the sound of the saw and the smell of wood that was flowing out from the workshop, together with the sun and grass. Meanwhile, I was able to draw or paint something. I liked that, too.

Urban and the old man appeared in the doorway of the old barn and they came directly toward me. The old man reached out his hand, warm with work, and said his name was Gertig He said he was so happy to meet me, that Urban had told him that we are getting married this year. That came as news to me! But I kept a straight face. The old man went on and said that Urban and I were going to have lunch with him and his wife now. She knew what food Urban liked, and she often made it for him when he came around.

This was a real treat for me. The farmhouse was one of those you wish you could go into and look around. All the things inside were very old, as old as the house. The doors were small, and there was an open fireplace and a wood-burning stove. And the interesting thing was that, not too long ago, there had also been cows living in half of the kitchen! There was only a thin wall put up with an opening; many farmhouses had only half a wall. All for the heat! Now there were only two cows, and they were outside.

The Gertigs spoke Bavarian, and I needed Urban to translate. Mrs. Gertig was a sweet old lady. She wore a typical long dress and an apron. (Mrs. Gertig, with her geese, would later be in one of my favourite paintings.) She stood by the stove, smiling warmly. She said she hoped that we were hungry, because she knew that Urban was helping her husband, and she had made Urban's favourite meal, *Dampf Nudeln* with vanilla sauce. I had no idea what it was, and no idea now either! It looked like a humungous noodle, with lots of vanilla sauce poured over it. It was good!

Later, Urban and I walked up the hill on the other side of Mother's house. There were a lot of hills in this place. There were also a lot of fields, and it was absolutely beautiful. We walked along a narrow, winding, gravel road. In front of us was another old farmhouse. When we came closer, we saw it was a bigger farm, probably over a hundred years old. It was as pretty as a picture. There were geese running around, and a horse looked out of a window in the house! (That would also become one of my favourite paintings.)

Down a little steep hill was another beautiful old stock house. It had been made into a restaurant and a small hotel. We met the owners, two men, who were very nice and friendly. Inside, the restaurant was beautifully decorated with pretty tablecloths and flowers on every table. You could also eat outside on a big patio. We sat down there. The view was incredible! We could see seven church towers from where we sat! Urban and I each had a coffee before we wandered back again.

Mother was sitting outside on the other side of the house, in the sun. We told her that we had eaten with the Gertigs, and she thought that was nice. Then she said she had something to talk to me about. I said okay, and she said we should go inside and talk about it, where we would be alone.

CHAPTER 19

THE SURPRISE

I followed Mother into the house. It was nice and cool in the hallway. We went in to the living room, and she motioned for me to take a seat on the corner bench.

She started at once, saying, "Birgit, Urban loves you very much. The only thing he talks is about is you, and how much he loves you. Do you love him?"

That was a direct question. I almost got angry, but I was also a bit puzzled, so I answered, "Yes, I do."

"Good," said Mother. Then she explained, "Urban has a court case from his time in the military. He was gone from the military for three days, and that is a criminal offence. Urban will go to Sweden with you, and stay until his case is concluded by the court. I will go to court for him, and tell them that he is not in the country, and what a hard life he had growing up. And that he, as a matter of fact, of his own free will, reported himself after the war. I am going to write to your parents and ask them."

I was stunned! I don't really remember what else she talked about. But the point was, Urban was going with me to Stockholm, and I didn't really know if I liked the idea.

I liked Urban. He was caring, funny, and had all the qualities I had in mind for a future boyfriend or husband: blond, wore glasses, smart, and strong enough to carry me. And the most important thing, that he not be too handsome, that other girls would take him. He also had to be a good dancer. No good dancer, no boyfriend for me.

Urban had all these qualities, but what would my parents say? Honestly, I did not have any thoughts of bringing home a boyfriend from Germany, like a souvenir. If things would have developed into real love, that I could not live without him, my parents certainly would have sent for him. But as things stood, I was not too sure myself that it was really love.

CHAPTER 20

HOME TO STOCKHOLM

Things were not going my way. But Urban was very happy! Urban had told all the people we met in the village that we were going to marry this year. This news must have reached his sisters, who, strangely enough, said to me on separate occasions, "Birgit, don't marry Urban." I, of course, didn't think anything of it. Urban hadn't even asked me!

The days went by quickly, and soon we were saying goodbye to Mother and Uncle Max at the train station. It was not that fun to have Urban as a travel companion; he was already homesick, and we were not even in Hamburg!

Nearing Gedser , I could already smell the water; then I saw the boats and heard the seagulls screaming, and I got kind of a free feeling. But I didn't know I had a surprise coming.

We were on the boat, about to enter Denmark. Passports had to be shown, and the usual questions were asked when crossing into another country. I showed my passport, then Urban showed his. What was that? I looked over at Urban's passport as the customs officer opened it. I was shocked to see another last name, Ohms, not von Schlosshof, as Urban had told me his name was.

Urban said, a little bit embarrassed, "I thought you knew, Mother was married before the war. Uncle Max is not our father. But he is going to adopt me and my youngest sister, and afterwards we are going to have Uncle's name. The adoption is soon to be finished."

CHAPTER 21

MEETING PAPPA

The train rolled slowly in to Copenhagen Central station. It stopped with a jerk and the sound of heavy chains swinging. We had taken down our luggage, and stood ready by the door. Urban opened the door and carried our luggage out to the platform. I jumped down, and looked around. Pappa and Uncle Gösta, who were coming to meet us, should be somewhere. Uncle Gösta was tall like a flag pole, so he would be easy to spot.

Suddenly, I heard Pappa's voice shouting, "My daughter, it's my daughter!" And he came running across the platform with his arms wide open. He lifted me and twirled me around before he put me down. He hugged me and kissed me and laughed, with tears in his eyes. What a welcome! I have never had such a feeling of being loved, before or after.

We made introductions. Uncle Gösta spoke German well, Pappa not so well. But he made up new words in German, in talking to me and to Urban at the same time. Pappa was so happy.

We boarded the night train to Stockholm. After we had eaten dinner in the dining car, we looked for our beds. I slept very well on trains. Dunkedy-dunkedy-dunk ... you could almost make a song of the wheels on the track.

"Stockholm Central next," the conductor called out, as he went through every car. I was excited to be home again. The people looked different, even the smell was different! It was still early morning, and the air was a bit humid. I listened to the sounds of rattling train cars echoing, voices over the speakers, and the hum of people coming and going. It was nice, and I took all of it in. It was time to say thank-you and goodbye to Uncle Gösta, and take a taxi home.

The taxi stopped at our building, right in the middle of a hill. We climbed out of the taxi, took the suitcases, paid the fare, and stood in front of "my" house. I was happy to be home.

We took the elevator to the third floor. My heart was beating a bit faster. Any minute now, I would be seeing Mamma again. Mamma must have heard the elevator, because she had opened the door, and was standing there, smiling in welcome. Mamma hugged and kissed me, and even Urban got a warm welcome. Mamma spoke German, so there was no language problem.

The table was set for breakfast. The sun was shining in, and everything was light. There were flowers on the table. Urban was not as talkative as usual, but then again, he couldn't speak Swedish.

After breakfast, we began talking business, that is, where Urban would be staying or living for the time he was here, if there was time set when he was going home, and whether he had a return ticket.

He told us Mother had only bought him a one way ticket, because it was cheaper to buy a new ticket than an open return ticket. Mother would tell him when he should go home.

The first few nights he slept at our place. It was not a big apartment, and it was impractical to have guests sleep over. So Mamma started to look in the paper for a room for rent for Urban, and she found one with a family that was not that close to us; Urban would have to take the subway to come to us.

It did not seem that Mother was in rush to get Urban home. My mother went with Urban to get a work permit, but he was denied.

His application for a visa to stay was denied too. He was fine to stay for three months, without a visa.

I did not like how Mother treated Urban, or for that matter, my parents. They chipped in with money for Urban while he was not getting any work. Finally he got a dishwashing job at a restaurant on Kungs gatan, and he also washed windows. I was in school again, and Urban picked me up from school every day.

Urban was introduced to my relatives on Pappa's side of the family; they were all in Stockholm. He met my five cousins, three of Pappa's sisters, and one brother. They were all very close to their parents, my grandparents.

My parents and I took Urban to Orsa, in north Sweden, to introduce him to Mamma's family. He met Mamma's sister Ingrid and her husband Sven, and their sons Ove and Åsa. He also met my grandfather; my grandmother was dead.

On Saturday night, we all went dancing at a Folk parkThere were a lot of people that we knew. I told Urban to go and dance with the women. He did, and there was one woman who spoke German. Urban told her what a misery it was trying to get a work visa and visa to stay in Sweden. The woman told Urban her husband was the chief of police in Orsa, and that he would help him.

At nine o'clock Monday morning, Urban went to the police station with his passport. At 9:30 he walked out, holding his passport stamped with a work visa and visa to stay. Urban was happy, to say the least! That meant that now he could look for work in his line. The police chief was so nice. He told Urban that his wife had told him what a hard time he had getting the visas. He stamped the passport so Urban would never need to have it renewed.

Meanwhile, Urban and I had fights now and then, and that was scary. Urban got so mad one time, that he banged his head on the wall of a building when we were outside. I told myself, he is all alone here and has nobody except for me; he probably would rather be home. I'm sure he'll be better once he gets more familiar with us. My God, where is Mother?

And then, a real shocker: I was pregnant.

CHAPTER 22

ENGAGEMENT

Pappa looked lost. Mamma looked like a firebomb about to explode.

"You are going to have a baby? When?" she cried.

"Well I'm not exactly sure," I said. "In the early spring, I think." But I really did not know.

"What are you going to do now? What about school? We just paid for you to go to school!" I was going to Bergs Commercial Art School, and was studying to become a commercial artist. I thought I at least had the foundation, and I was pretty good at fashion drawing.

"I know, but I am quitting," I said. "And we are planning to get married." Meanwhile, Urban did not say a word.

Pappa said, "You don't have to get married, you know, Birgit. Lots of people don't marry. We can surely find a way, any way."

"No," I said. "We will get married. It is the right thing to do, if you have a baby."

We got engaged on Urban's birthday. My Aunt Ingrid had even come down to Stockholm from Orsa. We had a little engagement party.

Pappa had bought our engagement rings. They were just so beautiful! They were 22 karat gold, with a band of flowers.

I don't remember what we were talking about, but it came up that I should iron Urban's shirt. I put my foot down and said, "I am not going to iron any shirt! We are not married yet!"

"Urban, where is the shirt? I'll iron it for you," my Aunt Ingrid said.

She ironed the shirt in front of the guests. Urban was angry. He slammed down the engagement ring, and it rolled off the table. Before anybody could stop it, the ring rolled onto the balcony and over the balcony edge, and it landed in the flower box of the people in floor below.

Urban had to go down there himself and say, "I'm sorry, can I pick up my engagement ring from your flower box?" He must have felt pretty dumb. Serves him right, I thought.

For the next couple of days, we planned the wedding. We thought that we would get married in Sofia church in my community, and where I had been confirmed.

We went to the church office and told them our plans. The banns had to be published in the church four Sundays in a row before we could get married. That means the community has to know that you are planning to marry. It is an old tradition, but it was mandatory.

We agreed, but upon consideration, Urban did not have a real job yet, so we decided to go to Germany and get married there, but it was not as easy as we had thought.

We went to a city called Braunschweig, halfway between Stockholm and Munich. Urban's birth father was living here with his family. We visited him a couple of times, and he had also visited my parents. After a week, I had to go back to Stockholm because we could not rent a room together, since we were not married.

Urban got us an appointment to get married in the courthouse on December 29, 1959, just six months after we had met in Munich. I was thinking of the movie, *One Summer of Happiness* with Ulla Jacobsson. Well that was me.

My parents and I went down to Braunschweig the day before the wedding. Mamma had sewn my dress, an ice-blue duchess-style dress, very pretty. I had designed it myself. I also had to go to the hairdresser before I got married.

Queen Farah Diba was very popular at the time. Everybody copied her hairstyle. I hated it, but that was exactly what I got! My hair was tested to the hilt. I should have done my hair myself.

Then we went to a photographer. Urban in a suit and me in my ice-blue dress. I had gotten a beautiful wedding bouquet from Urban, pink roses and lily of the valley.

Our wedding was done by the Justice of the Peace, and the witness was just somebody from the hall. The guests were Mother and Urban's sister Sabine, and my mother and father. When the judge took for granted that I would be a German citizen I said no, and I remained a Swedish citizen.

Pappa had ordered brunch at the hotel where we were staying. It was beautifully decorated, and there was a big cake! We could not eat all of the food, there was so much. The leftovers were sent to an orphanage in the city.

The next night my parents, Urban, and I took the night train to Munich. Mother and Sabine had already left right after the brunch, in Mother's car.

We got seats on the train to Munich; it wasn't too far. The four of us were the only ones in the compartment. The heat system broke down halfway through the trip, and the compartment was ice-cold. I don't know how we survived, but I took all my heat from Urban.

Finally, in Munich, we took a taxi, with heat! We went from Munich to the village where Mother lived.

CHAPTER 23

TUTZING

Urban's mother had been looking for an apartment for us, and had found one in Tutzing. It was approximately thirty minutes away from her place, on the other side of Lake Starnberg.

I had never heard of Tutzing, but apparently it was known for a political school of some kind. We went to look. It was a private house that rented out a basement apartment. It had two rooms and a kitchen. There was a grass lawn that we could use, and private entrance. We said we'd take it. My parents were going to pay for the rent and the telephone. Mother was going for the food.

We moved in. I don't think we had anything more than an orange-and-white rug that my grandmother in Orsa had woven for me, and a picture that I got from one of Pappa's friends with an easel the painting rested on.

But the apartment was not empty for long. Urban was handy and had lots of ideas. He made a free-hanging bookshelf of ropes and small planks. He made a bench with planks and bricks and dressed it with material he had gotten from Mother. That was our sofa. For a lamp, Urban painted a big hotdog can red, and made lots of holes in it for light to shine through. There was no bottom on the can, so it was light and bright.

We put the lamp on a coffee table Urban had made and placed my grandmother's woven rug underneath. Beautiful!

My parents come visiting again. They brought us a bed, pots and pans, and other things we needed.

It was almost spring, and the weather was very nice and warm. My parents, Urban, and I went for a walk down by the lake. There was a ten-metre-high tower on the beach, to jump from. Not a soul was around, other than us. Urban decided he was going to show off. He was going to let us know what a good swimmer he was. He got undressed down to only his underwear, then he climbed up the tower, stood up there for a few seconds, and jumped!

Everything went fine. A proud Urban, shaky from being in the ice-cold water, ran to his mother- and father-in-law and his disbelieving wife.

It was time for a strong whisky for Pappa, and a strong coffee for the rest of us. We really needed it after that very eventful walk on the beach.

My mother fried fish for dinner. I took a bite, stopped, and looked at the others. They were not chewing either. It was awful! Mamma could not believe it! But Urban showed his gentlemanly side, and to save the situation said, "It must be sweetwater fish. This is different than what we are used to!" But no, Mamma had been frying the fish in sugar! The packaging looked the same as the salt package. *Guten Appetit!*

CHAPTER 24

WAITING FOR BABY

We had gone to the only doctor we could find in Tutzing. He was very nice. I had not been gaining much weight. Urban and I went walking every day, and we thought that it would make the baby come sooner.

Meanwhile, we lived quite well in our little home. Urban had gotten a job making caskets. Lucky for us, there were a lot of elderly people in Tutzing. He also helped with placing the body into the casket.

We did not need much money for food; we bought mostly canned food, or Knorr soups out of a bag.

We had also gotten a kitten named Andersson. Then we got two bunnies, Olivia and Tango. We were a happy family. The three of them slept in my arms: bunny, cat, bunny. I don't think that Andersson dared to move.

One day an older man come to visit us. Urban knew him; he was Mother's father-in-law, Mr. von Schlosshof Sr. He was living in Tutzing, and had gotten our address from Mother.

Everybody in Mother's family called him Opa, and he was a wonderful man. He visited us about once a week. Once, I saw him coming, and he was holding something behind his back. He knocked at the door, and when I opened it, he took a beautiful bouquet of flowers from behind his back. He gave them to me, and at the same time, reached into the bag he also was holding and said, "I figured you wouldn't have a vase, so I brought one with me!"

And one day he came wearing a very nice outfit. I told him he looked nice, and he said, "This is my old duck hunting suit. It has been a long time since I've worn it, but I thought you might like it."

Opas .father had been a conductor. He had conducted the first performance of *Der Rosenkavalier* in Dresden. His father had also been knighted by Kaiser Franz Joseph of Austria.

In all, we were pretty happy with our lives. We did not fight that much. Although, I had never heard my parents say a single word in a harsh tone to each other, so disagreements over nothing was new to me.

One day, it was just that. I don't know if I had said something, or what started it. Suddenly, Urban got really mad, reached for a hammer, and threw it at me! I don't know if he meant to hit me, or only scare me. I was stiff with fear, and I was near the bed, so I just lay down. Urban screamed something and went out.

I suddenly remembered I had sleeping pills from the doctor in case I had a hard time sleeping. I had never taken any, but now I thought I needed to sleep. So I took one. I did not fall asleep, so I took another one, and another one, until like finally I felt strange. Urban came in and said something to me, then he called his mother. I just thought, *let me sleep.*

Urban and Mother forced me up. They told me I had to walk in the fresh air. They held me under each arm and dragged me. It did not work. I heard them saying they had to take me to the hospital. At this point, I just wanted to sleep.

The hospital was a sterile place with white tiles on half the walls and it echoed when people were speaking. I think the nurses was nuns. They were wearing cornflower blue uniform dresses with white aprons. They put me in a chair, and tied a big rubber apron around me. Then they came with a rubber hose that looked like a garden hose. They put one end in my mouth and told me to swallow. I heard Mother tell them to be careful, that I was going to have a baby very soon.

I don't know if I swallowed, or if they pushed the hose the whole way down to my stomach. I threw up everything. It was the worst experience I had ever had, and I would never take a sleeping pill again. I have never told anybody of this terrible experience, nor was I ever reminded of it by Mother or Urban. It was like it never happened. No one ever knew this story of my life, until now.

CHAPTER 25

BIRTH AND BAPTISM

Urban kissed and hugged me, and I understood that he was sorry. I was confused; is this what it is like to be married? I didn't know about any marriages other than my parents. I sometimes though that we could always divorce, but that it would not be good even to try. But as a security blanket, it was good to know.

My doctor told me he would be going on vacation for two weeks, and when he returned it would be time for my baby to be born.

We got to borrow a nice bassinet from the midwife. Everything seemed to be in order until the midwife called and told us she had yellow fever! And the doctor had left for vacation. Well, let's hope she would be better when it was time for the baby to be born.

Shortly after midnight, I tapped on Urban's back and told him I thought the baby would be coming soon. By morning, no baby had come. Urban went to the hospital on a bike. Mother had come, so I was not alone. Urban soon returned with a tub, and in it was everything he needed for a home birth.

The day turned into evening. Urban was trying everywhere, to see if he could get a hold of a doctor. Finally he found a retired doctor who agreed to help us deliver the baby. He told Urban to call him when it the time came close.

Mother had to leave. My sister-in-law Elsa, married to Urban's oldest brother Dirk, was expecting their second baby at the same time as me. They already had a two-year-old son, Bob. Elsa was the same age as me.

Urban had made me a bed, and there was a tub from the hospital to put my bum on. There was a lightbulb hanging from the ceiling, giving strong light.

The retired doctor had come, and he stood waiting with his thumbs in his suspenders. Finally, ten minutes before midnight, Gunnar was born! Weighing more than ten pounds, he was big like a one-month-old.

The doctor sewed me up, everything had been done without any anesthesia. Urban had been a good assistant; the midwife could not have done better. Urban had to clean and wash me, as I was exhausted.

The doctor left, and Urban and I and our baby son were alone. Urban read about how to bathe a newborn baby. He used a little of the water that we had been boiling all day long. Why do you have to boil water, almost until the wallpaper rolls down off the walls?

Urban held the baby under the arms, exactly as he should, and I looked proudly on. Splash! Gunnar went under the water! Urban quickly fished him up, and the baby did not make a peep! Soon he was clean, dry, and dressed.

Elsa, my sister-in-law, gave birth the same night, only ten minutes past midnight, to twins! A boy and a girl.

My parents were going to come. They were excited and happy to hear that everything had gone well. They had been so worried when I told them I was going to have a home birth. That was from my grandmother's time. Nobody in Sweden had a baby at home these days.

I had a hard time walking after Gunnar was born. My muscles had been torn while pushing during the birth. It was a week before I could walk again. Urban had a lot to do, with washing diapers and baby bottles, and I was limited help. Mamma's girlfriend, Gun, came to help.

Gunnar was almost a week old when our doctor returned from his holiday. He was surprised but very happy that both baby and mother were well.

Mother said we had to get rid of our little family of bunnies and the cat. She said the hair, especially from the cat, was dangerous to the baby. So, we gave the animals to a farmer nearby, with a few tears.

One day Urban wanted to go to Munich by himself. He was going to see his old girlfriend, Beate, whom he had dated before we met. She did not know that he was married now, or that he had a baby. As if that was so important. I had met her once, and I did not like her. Why did he have to go and meet her? But he went. He did not seem to care, or even to notice, that I was a bit heartbroken over that. I did not carry grudges, but I remembered.

Life went along in our little home. Mamma cooked, Gun cleaned, and we were making plans to baptize Gunnar.

Mamma brought us the baptismal gown that she had worn when she was baptized in 1919. Now it was 1961.

Gunnar was baptized on a beautiful, sunny spring day in a small church in Tutzing. Our invited guests numbered slightly more than those at our wedding. Gunnar was so sweet, he was a beautiful baby in my mother's baptismal gown. He didn't even cry when the minister poured the water on his head and gave him my father's name, Gunnar Jürgen. Opa was the godfather.

The days went by quickly, and Mamma and Gun had made a plan for us. They told Urban and me that we probably would have it better in Stockholm. Urban could get work, and we would be nearer to doctors.

Yes, it probably was a good idea. We were going to live with my parents until Urban got a job.

The days remaining before we left for Stockholm were busy. We had to get Gunnar a passport. We had to get rid of all our things we could not take with us to Sweden, like my grandmother's rug. Sabine got that. We said goodbye to our cat and bunnies at the farm. I don't know if they remembered us.

I lay down in the long grass, Urban beside me, holding my hand. Gunnar was sleeping. It was near the end of our stay in Germany, in Tutzing, and I was a little sad, after all we had been through there. Urban squeezed my hand said, "It will be okay in Stockholm, too. We just have to find an apartment. I love you."

CHAPTER 26

TIBRO, SWEDEN

Mamma, Gun, and I flew to Stockholm with Gunnar. Urban would come in a few days, after he had gotten rid of our things and cleaned the apartment.

Once again, we had to live with my parents. That arrangement was not really good, and there was no real work for Urban, either.

One day, while my parents were gone up north, we looked in the paper, and what did we see? There was an ad for a cabinet maker in Tibro! I had never heard of the place, and had no idea where it was.

There was a telephone number, and we called. We could come today, but we had to take the train. Tibro was about three hours south of Stockholm by train.

We got dressed, took Gunnar in his light blue carrier, and off we went to the railway station. Urban had called the workplace before we went to the train, so now they awaited us. We went with high hopes.

Finally, we arrived, and Urban was hired on the spot. We had not known that Tibro was where most of the furniture in Sweden was manufactured.

We moved to Tibro the following week. Urban's employer found an apartment for us on the second floor of a private home.

The landlords were an older couple, and they offered us a baby carriage. It was beautiful: dark blue, with enormous wheels, like a prince's carriage.

There was nothing special about Tibro. I took Gunnar for a walk every day, and we always saw this old horse. Somebody said that he was a mean horse. I decided we were going to fix that. So every day when we went by, I had the baby carriage, with Gunnar in it, full of fresh long grass for the horse. The horse was so happy, and waited for us every day.

New apartment buildings were being built, and we went to look at them. They were nice, two-storey apartments, with a balcony. The kitchen and living room were downstairs and the bedrooms were upstairs, with an open staircase from the living room. We got a two bedroom apartment with a balcony.

Then there was the furniture. Needless to say, Urban chose the best of the best. Urban made good money in Tibro, but for the furniture we took out a loan. He bought light grey club chairs and a dark grey sofa. Our tables and cabinets were all teak wood and the textiles were by Viola Gråsten. It was quite nice. We got a new vacuum cleaner, too.

There is a story about the new vacuum cleaner. I was putting groceries away in the kitchen one day, when I dropped a package of sugar on the floor. The package broke, and the sugar spilled out. I thought I had better get it cleaned up before Urban got home. I got out the new vacuum, put the hose in, and turned it on. But to my great surprise, the sugar flew all over the kitchen floor! I ran after it with the hose, but the sugar just went running away! Just then Urban came home. He looked at me, he looked at the vacuum cleaner, and said, "What are you doing?" I told him I had spilled sugar on the floor, and now I'm trying to vacuum it up.

Urban took the vacuum from me and looked at the white stuff that I had managed to spread all over the kitchen floor. He took the hose out and put on in the other end of the vacuum cleaner. And it sucked.

Winter came, and it started to get colder. Tibro is flat, and the wind whipped around over the big fields. It was not a pretty or interesting city anyway, so when Urban suggested moving back to Stockholm, I was all for it. Urban's job was not challenging, even though he earned enough. I had met no girlfriends; I only knew the neighbour lady.

Before we left for Stockholm, we thought we would go dancing on a Saturday night. We asked a friend if he would babysit Gunnar. He said yes, and I made plans for what to wear.

Saturday came. We took a taxi, because we did not have a car. The place was full. The band had started playing, and we finally got to the coat check, paid, and got the receipt. Guys were going around, checking out the girls they wanted to dance with. We elbowed ourselves in, closer to the stage. I had almost forgotten what it was like in dance clubs. The noise from the people mixed with the music and the smoke was like a thick rug lying over everything. I had thought we were going to enjoy the evening, but I felt lost.

Urban and I danced, and some other people mixed with us sometimes. I noticed Urban dancing with the same girl, dance after dance. Finally, it came to the last dance of the evening, and the bandleader announced the last dance.

The last dance is usually with the girl or guy you go home with, or plan to see again. I turned to Urban, but he stared past me, pushed me a bit to the side, and went, without looking at me, to the girl that I had seen him dancing with throughout the evening. And there they were, close to each other, cheek to cheek. Urban didn't give me a glance, did not even see me. I felt like a little bird that could not fly, sitting in the corner with a broken wing.

I had to wait for Urban to give his new girlfriend her coat first, to help her put on her coat, say good night, and give her a kiss on the cheek, before he helped me. The car ride home was silent. I was crushed.

The next day was Sunday, and I was bathing Gunnar in the bathtub. He was so adorable, and I called Urban to come look how cute Gunnar was in the bathtub with his rubber duck. No answer. I called out again, and our friend showed up and said, "I just drove Urban to a girl's house, the one he met yesterday. He took his drawings with him to show her."

Urban had taken my drawings and paintings to tell people that he had done them! I just stood there, stunned. I did not know what to say, I just wanted to cry. How could he? But I just thanked our friend for letting me know.

I was heartbroken. Urban had not drawn one single line, and I have signed them all "Ohms," so he was passing them off as his. That's the day I started to sign my pictures "B. Ohms."

We moved back to Stockholm later that week, and I thought then that I would never get over this. I had no idea what was waiting for me.

CHAPTER 27

UPPLANDS VÄSBY

We had to live with my parents for a long time. Urban could not get any work, so we also went to Orsa for a while, but there it was even worse.

I was pregnant again. My mother almost passed out when I told her. Since there was nothing she could do, she had to live with it. We had already given the new baby a name, Thona, after my beloved grandmother in Orsa. She had passed away when I was sixteen. We were certain the baby would be a girl, but of course we did not know.

Urban wanted to take Gunnar home to his mother, and show her Gunnar, now over a year old. Mamma and Pappa thought they should go with them to Copenhagen on the train. Then Urban would go on the night train to Munich. That would be easier for him with Gunnar.

It was August. I went to the station with Urban, Gunnar, and my parents. I waved to them as they left on the train. Urban was happy, they were going to be gone for two weeks. And when he came back, it would be time for me to have the baby. We had asked the doctor when the baby would be born.

I stood there and watched the train disappear with my whole family. Was that a small ache I just felt? I went to my grandmother's home, so I would not be alone. I went to bed, and woke up after midnight. It was time to call a taxi.

Thona arrived! She was smaller than Gunnar, weighing just over eight pounds, and had tricolour hair: black, red, and white. It wasn't a lot of hair, only a few strands. Gunnar did not have any hair when he was born.

Soon after Thona was born, Urban found work in a furniture manufacturer in Upplands Väsby. Somewhat closer to Stockholm than Tibro, it was only one hour north, near Uppsala. There was even a small, one bedroom house for rent, not far from the factory. We felt very lucky. We took all our furniture out of storage, where it had been ever since we moved from Tibro.

Now we were starting over, but with two kids, and I liked it. But we didn't go a week without a fight. I don't even know what we always fought about. But at one dinner I had had enough. Urban was complaining about onion sauce! I got so mad that I threw the onion sauce at him. It landed on the ceiling above the kitchen door, where it still was when we later moved! I never served onion sauce again.

I don't know what it was with that house, but it didn't bring us any luck. I had bad eczema on my hands, so that the doctor had said I needed someone to help with washing around the house. I had a woman who would come in every day and help me with the dishes, bathe Thona, and she also cooked a bit.

I had a habit of putting my gold bracelet in a flowerpot in the windowsill every night. One morning I reached for it, but it was not there. It was not anywhere. My heart stood still. Had I lost my gold bracelet with its many charms?

Urban had to go to Stockholm that morning, and I was afraid of what he was going to say.

So I told him when he came in the evening. He said that Mrs. Andersson, the woman who came to help me, must have taken it, and that I should ask her not to come anymore, that I did not need her help anymore. I was sad to see her go. She had been kind of a buffer between us. Urban could not say anything bad to me when she was around.

We had no neighbours. Up the street was a house, but that was a bit away and I had never seen anybody at that house. Down the street was the highway, and across it, the factory where Urban worked. To the right, only fields, and to the left a bit farther was a police station.

We had friends from Stockholm that came and visited us sometimes, and my parents came almost every weekend. Urban painted a lot during that time. He used a lot of black in his paintings. I think he was trying to imitate Kokoschka, who used a lot of black in his drawings and paintings. I never liked his art.

One day Urban come home from work and asked what I had done all day. I told him that I had been cleaning and dusting. We stood out in the hall, and he lifted his arm, and brushed his fingers against the top of the door frame. "You have not cleaned here," he said, and smeared the dirt in my face. I was sad, hurt, and angry. I never forgot to dust on top of the door frames again.

The days went on, and Urban was making us a pretty bench of white iron, with a pink stuffed seat with white nails. He liked to make nice things for us.

One evening, I don't know what set him off. He got so angry, almost mad. He started yelling at me, and was foaming at the mouth. He went berserk, turning chairs upside down, then the table and sofa, all as if he had lost it completely. I stood and tried to get out when he turned his back to pull down the drapes. I ran for the door and out into the dark.

I was barefoot, but I did not feel it, I was so scared. There was a crust on the snow, I ran on top of the snow, like I was flying. I ran to the police station, and banged on the door. Nothing happened, nothing moved. Although the lights were on, the door was locked.

I turned around, and ran home. I knew that Urban would never hurt the kids. The door was still open; Urban was quiet and had started to clean up his mess. I went through the kitchen to the bedroom. Thona and Gunnar were sleeping, and I crawled into bed and must have slept.

Urban whispered my name. "Honey, get up. I have a surprise." I really would rather have slept. But I got up, and went to the living room.

He had set a small table with two coffee cups and candles. And in front of it all stood a freshly painted painting. The living room was orderly again, he had painted a new painting, made coffee, and lit candles. Everything was nice. He didn't say "I'm sorry," he never did, but we enjoyed the peace for the moment.

We still argued, at least once a week. That is, Urban argued. He often punched me on my upper arms, as if I were a punching bag. I was just grateful that he did not punch me in the face.

I once said to him that maybe he should go talk to a psychiatrist, since he gets so angry so often. But no, there was nothing wrong with him he said.

It seems that I am telling about all the bad moments, but we had very nice moments too, of course, where we laughed, and were not fighting.

When Urban came home from work one evening, he was angry with me again. I don't recall what it was about. But I remember this very well: he took my head in his two hands, placed his thumbs on my eyelids, and said in a threatening voice, "I am going to push in your eyes!" He pushed and I screamed, broke loose, and ran for the front door.

I didn't make it. He grabbed me hard by the arm, dragged me back, and showed me a knife, a big kitchen knife. He pushed me to go out, but I was not willing, and I fell. Then he got a grip on my hair and was going to pull me by my hair up the street. Again I screamed.

"You can scream as much as you want to, nobody will hear you! Get up!" I stood up, crying and freezing. He was holding the knife. Then suddenly he said, "Go!" And we went inside.

There was no explanation, no apology. It was never mentioned again, like all the other times. We never said anything about it. It was like it had never happened.

In winter in Sweden, the days are short and the nights are long. We are in darkness much of the time. Finally, it began to get lighter outside. Green grass was coming up. Trees and bushes started to bud, and birds were chirping after a long and cold winter. Even a lone dizzy fly landed on a sunny window sill.

Thona was going to be baptized, and we had found the perfect church. It was a Lutheran church, and was the tiniest church I had ever seen. The story goes that a well-to-do farmer was going to marry off his only daughter, but all the churches in the neighbourhood were busy, so he set out to build one himself. It had thick outer walls, and inside it was all white. The middle aisle was narrow, and on both sides were rows of benches, for two people each. There was a pulpit for the priest, and room for baptism. It even had a tower with a bell, and stained glass windows.

Thona was baptized in Yttergrans Commun in Upplands Väsby. It was a sunny day, and we had a few guests. My aunt, Pappa's youngest sister, was godmother. Thona wore my mother's baptismal gown from 1919, as Gunnar had too.

My parents had meanwhile found us a little apartment in Stockholm. It had one bedroom, a small kitchen, and bath. Urban's job had not been much, and we were happy to move to civilization again.

CHAPTER 28

LILLA ESSINGEN

The apartment in Lilla Essingen was so small we hardly had room for furniture. Thona slept in a wicker basket on the washing machine and Gunnar slept in the bathtub. But when asked, Urban always said it was him that slept in the bathtub. I had made a bed for Gunnar, so it was soft and nice.

The view from our window was a stone wall. It was dark and boring inside, so I was outside as much as I could with the kids. Essingen was also not a very interesting place. Urban had gotten work on Stora Essingen. Essingen was two islands that were connected with a long, high bridge. I really don't know what his job was; there were only ships and a harbour there.

My girlfriend Märta came to visit one day. She was a nurse. She was very disturbed when Urban wouldn't let Gunnar walk on the rug. Gunnar was two years old, and he was only allowed to walk on the floor. And Urban was also angry at me because he thought that I was too nicely dressed. He got really mad, and Märta tried to calm him down.

One day I got a letter from Mother. I did not really understand what she wrote, and I was sure she had wrongly understood something I had written. I would have to show Urban when he comes home, I thought.

However, as I remember, I had not been writing to her, I had been writing to Ullie. But Mother opens all the letters and reads them, especially if they are not addressed to her, I found out later. And if you wrote a letter at her house and forgot it on the desk, she read that, too.

I showed Urban the letter I had received from his mother. I should not have done that, but I was so naïve, and I didn't believe she meant any harm, or was mad at me. Once again I was wrong, and Urban became furious. Again his mouth was foaming and he hissed since he could not scream, and I felt the punch hanging in the air. I was afraid, and since I happened to be standing by the door, I turned the key and out I went. I ran down the stairs and out into the street.

What was going to happen when I went back? No, I was not going back now. The kids were safe with him.

I waved down a taxicab. I did not have any money on me, but I gave the driver my parents' address. My father would come down to him with the money. I had slippers on.

It was a long drive, and finally the taxi stopped at my parents' address. I went up the stairs, and rang the doorbell. I heard Pappa's footsteps in the hall. He opened the door and he smiled, surprised to see me. l explained quickly why I was there, and he ran down and paid the nice taxi driver.

I stood inside the door and got a warm feeling, smelling the familiar pipe and cigar smells from Pappa's smoking. Mamma was equally surprised to see me, and was happy that I came. She made coffee, and we sat down to drink. The telephone rang, and I said if it is Urban, I didn't want to talk to him. Mamma said I should just talk to him, but I refused.

Pappa had a good friend who was a police chief, and Pappa said he was going to call him and ask him for a little help. Pappa wanted to ask him if he could send somebody out to check on Urban.

The police chief at once sent two police officers, one woman and one man. They reported back that Urban had just been feeding the kids. The kids looked good, healthy, and clean. No trauma. They had been talking for a long while with Urban, who said he wanted his wife to come home.

The next day, the police called and told us that a social worker had gone and checked on Urban and the kids, and she would go back again. An appointment had been set up for Urban and me tomorrow, and the social worker would then take our kids to the country for two weeks. He said it was a beautiful, peaceful place and while the children were there, the two of us would have time to think over what we were going to do. Stay together or get a divorce.

I told my parents I wanted to divorce Urban, but to my surprise Mamma said, "Where are you going to live then? You don't work and you have two kids. Pappa and I are working, and you cannot live here, especially with two kids!"

It sounded pretty cold, and I didn't know what to say. I only know if I met with Urban, I would automatically go back to him. And that was probably what my mother wanted. Not because she loved Urban, but because she did not know what to do. Neither did I, but I told myself I wouldn't be running to my parents with my problems soon again, if ever.

The next day we agreed to let the kids go to "summer camp." It was a big yellow manor, with white pillars. The air was clean and there were a lot of tall pine trees around. In the background I could see water glittering. It was a really beautiful place. We were told we could visit them any time.

Life returned to normal. Nothing was even whispered about what caused the big storm. The kids were back with us, and we avoided talking about what had happened. The only thing Urban had to say was, "If you or your parents make trouble again, I will immediately take a taxi and go to the German embassy, and fly to Germany with the children. They are German citizens."

CHAPTER 29

BONDEGATAN 1B

Our apartment was tiny,and dark,we did not ever had sunlight.

Mamma worked tirelessly to get another apartment for us. She found an ad in the paper saying that somebody wanted a small, one room apartment to exchange for an old, two bedroom apartment. The person was getting divorced. There was no money involved, just an exchange.

The apartment was on Bondegatan, my old street, and where my parents was still living. We could not believe our luck! Urban and I were happy, and so were my parents. The building was old; it still had wood stove, only cold running water, no heat, but it had a fireplace. There were porcelain stoves in the living room and bedrooms. There was a little electric stove in the kitchen, with two burners, so there was at least something to cook on. There was no refrigerator, but there was a pantry with ventilation to the outside, for storing food that needed to be kept cold. That's what was used before there were refrigerators.

The apartment was on the third floor, and there was no elevator. But that didn't matter, we thought. The apartment was big and beautiful. The ceilings were over nine feet high. I don't know exactly when it was built, but I would guess in the late 1920s.

I was so happy to be back in the city and hear the buzzing sound of traffic. All the conveniences were near. Next door was a small milk store. And right across on Götgatan, along with many other stores and a lot of movie theatres, was the big grocery store, Konsum.

On the corner of Bondegatan and Götgatan was a pub where mostly old men sat and drank beer. Then a framing store, and then our place, Bondegatan 1B.

My parents lived about twenty minutes up the street, by Sofia church. I had my friends and all my relatives on Pappa's side. I was back in the city that I grew up in!

Urban got a job right away, with a cabinet maker, and life seemed normal again. I went out every day, with Thona under one arm, and a blanket and toys under the other. I forever had to wait for Gunnar, because he did not want to walk. But he had to, and down we went, three floors down, where I had a wagon waiting.

We went up to Sofia church. There was a big green border all around the church, with big chestnut trees, park benches, and even a sandbox for kids. It was great. I also met other mothers there. I loved the big flowering chestnut trees. I brought a drawing book with me every day, so I could draw the kids in the sandbox while they played. That is, if I wasn't playing with them!

On the way home, we usually stopped by a candy store. We often met with my girlfriend from school. We have been friends ever since second grade. Maggan also had two kids, girls.

One day Maggan said, "Why don't you join the sewing club? We meet once a week, and it's all girls from Sofia School that you know, too. You can do knitting, or crocheting, or embroidery, anything!" I thought I would like to knit something for the kids, so I said I'd love to join.

I was happy to be gone one evening a week. It went well for a while, but Urban always met me on my way home. I had to say precisely what time I would be leaving the meeting, and he yelled at me if I was late.

Finally, I found it to be too much work, so I told Maggan that I would not come anymore.

It was summer again, and the kids and I went to Orsa. That was a lot of work with the kids. We had to hand wash everything, and make a fire in the fireplace, which I was soon doing like a professional. The house had no running water and we had to draw water from a well and carry it the whole way back. It was also a long way to the store. It was like living life a hundred years ago.

Urban had steady work in the city, and he came up every weekend, which was nice. Every weekend he had to take out all the slivers Thona had gotten in her feet during the week.

I had found a wooden cart to pull the kids around in, and they loved it. Every day we went down to the lake, them sitting in the cart. It was like in a storybook. The road went through the forest, and there was nobody other than me pulling the kids in blue-painted cart on the quiet road. We would stop on the side of the road, and the kids climbed out to pick blueberries. When their mouths, fingers, and feet were all blue, it was time to leave the blueberries and go down to the lake.

We could see the lake between the trees, blue and glittering in the sunlight. When we finally came to the lake, friends whom we saw every day were already there. The water was nice and warm by the shore where the kids played, but farther out it was ice-cold.

Summer was finished, and our time at Orsa came to an end. The train ride home was an adventure. Thona was walking. More than walking, she was climbing. She climbed up to where you put hats gloves and small items. There she lay down and slept!

Urban and my parents picking us up from the train station in Stockholm. Urban said he had a surprise to show us when we got home. I had no idea what it could be.

Walking the three flights up was easier than I remembered. We came inside the door, and to the right was the kitchen. I could see right away that something was different. Urban had redone the whole kitchen! The wood stove was gone, and it its place was a small kitchen table and an electric stove. The pantry was also gone, and instead there was a refrigerator. And there was hot water! My parents had bought us a small washing machine. I didn't know what to say; I was so happy and thankful.

Poor Urban had needed to carry the iron stove down the stairs himself, and the tiles behind and beside the stove also had to be carried down. That was a lot of heavy work to do alone.

More of my girlfriends started showing up. My cousin and her daughter, who was two years older than Gunnar, sometimes came to visit. Weekends we often went to my grandmother, Pappa's mother, called *farmor* in Swedish. Farmor lived in another area, called Wasa Stan, about one hour's walk from us. There were always aunts, uncles, and cousins at farmor's place. It was nice going to farmor's. She always made time for you, and always had the coffee ready. It a was warm and welcoming feeling.

We often walked over Riksbron where old men stood fishing from the bridge, and it was fun to watch them. My grandfather, *farfar* used to stand there fishing in the early mornings every day. He would catch fish every day, and brought the catch to home to farmor, who cleaned the fish and made different things for dinner.

My stomach started feeling a bit sick in the mornings. I knew in the back of my mind what that meant, but I would not listen. I refused to listen. I was pregnant. I felt doubly sick. Urban was good; he was always helpful and nice. My mother, however, looked anything but glad.

Meanwhile, we had made some friends in our building. Tom and Yvonne from downstairs, and Hans and Gunilla from the fourth floor, and Urban's best friend, Arne.

Arne's father was a tailor, and had even done tailoring for the king's house. Arne was at our place all the times, as he had a car repair shop nearby. I think that's how he and Urban met each another, not that we had a car, but Urban talked to anybody.

Arne, Urban, and another friend decided to go to Munich by car. It would take them two days to get there. They planned to stay with Urban's mother for about four days, then drive the two days home again.

The day they left, Arne came and gave me and the kids a big cake. I was a little upset to be left alone, but I had my parents within reach, should I need anything.

Everything went fine, and they had much to tell when they got home. Arne brought me flowers. Urban told me about the friend that went with them and what he had done in Hamburg on Reeperbahn. Reeperbahn is where all the "working girls" are. State controlled. Now I think that Urban was talking about himself. Anyway, they liked it at Urban's mother's place, and she liked Arne, too.

Summer came and the children and I went to Orsa again. Urban come up every weekend. This time the kids were running around more, and me with my big belly had a harder time catching them. But I still took them down to the lake in the blue cart every day.

Every day on the way to the lake, we stopped to pick and eat blueberries. And I was grateful that I never had to make bath water for the kids. They came out of the lake looking like raisins, and then we went home. It was a happy time.

We picked flowers one day in the field behind the house. I thought I would teach the kids the names of the flowers that we saw all time. So I started with buttercup. Thona looked at the bright yellow flower and said, "Mom, where is the cheese?" So much for the buttercup, she wanted the cheese, too.

That was a funny excursion, and not very long. They were not very interested to learn the names of flowers. I thought maybe they were too young.

Another funny incident happened one day when we went for the mail. The mailboxes were up the hill, between the birch trees. There was cars on the road once in a while, but also horses, mostly pulling a wagon full of hay. According to Gunnar, the horses were all girls. Because they had long hair!

Suddenly, a line of deer came out of the woods. I said, "Look!" And Thona said all enthusiastically, "That one! I want it! On wheels!"

We could not stay too long in Orsa, Just in case Pia (as we had been calling the baby) would come early. I would be having the baby in the same hospital where Thona was born. But this time Urban would be there.

Two weeks after I was back from Orsa, it was time to go to the hospital. Urban was there, rubbing my back and sniffing the laughing gas after every use. That was funny in itself.

Pia was born. The baby had a name already. She had the most of hair of the three of my babies, and it was blonde, almost white. She was also the smallest of the three at birth.

The event of the new baby, all the gifts, and the new kitchen, did not mean that all the fighting between Urban and I was over. No, that lived on. Many times it was about money. We had no money. Urban changed jobs often, and when we could not pay the rent I had to call the landlord, and it was very embarrassing for me. Urban never made such a call. A couple of times we had only candlelight because we could not pay the electricity bill.

Urban came late home often. I was sure that he was out with some girl. I could smell it when he came to bed beside me. It made me sick, thinking of it.

Soon it would be Christmas, but first was Lucia, a big feast day in Sweden. Someone representing Lucia is appointed, and a Lucia procession takes place on the streets everywhere. We used to go out and watch the Lucia procession, as did most people. But this year, Urban said he had to go someplace, and he would be home soon. So the kids and I watched the Lucia procession on TV.

I knew Urban was not with a friend; he was with a girl. I'm not stupid. I thought I would play detective. I checked his coat pockets and I found a streetcar receipt. It was clipped where he had disembarked. I knew the street, so I looked up the street name in the phone book. I picked a name and called the number. A man answered. He sounded friendly, and there was noise in the background. I asked to speak to Urban please. My heart was pounding. I was just taking a chance, if nobody with that name was there, I would excuse myself, saying I had the wrong number.

But to my sad surprise, the voice said, "Yes, just a second." And then he called out, "Urban, it's for you, it's Lucia!" And he laughed, not knowing who was really calling.

Urban came to the phone. In that moment, I hated him. I don't even remember what I said. It didn't matter; I might as well have hung up, because he came home with his tail between his legs.

Not long after that, I had just cleared the kitchen when the phone rang. When I answered, a young woman's voice said, "Is Urban there please?"

I said "No, he is at work."

She asked if she could have his number at work, and I said he was not reachable at work.

She said, "Who am I speaking with please?"

I said, "This is his wife."

Silence. Then crying. "I think I am pregnant. He says that he loves me, but he must be lying. He must love you. Do you have kids too?"

"Yes, three. The youngest one is three months."

More crying. The she said, "And he told me he lived with his sister." I felt sick.

CHAPTER 30

Annika was her name, and she came to see us. Urban wanted to disappear. *Serves him right*, I thought. Urban had gotten me a new bracelet to replace the one that had been stolen, and it was full of charms again. Annika looked at it and said, "Urban gave me the same Nefertiti charm."

It did not end there.

Urban and I had found a quiet studio to rent in Mosebacke. It was not far from home, and Urban could work on his big paintings there. Well, Urban had turned the studio into his and Annika's love nest. One day I went there and found a bed that I never seen before. Urban told me that Hans, our friend, used it for the girls his wife didn't know about. I did not believe him.

Urban, charmer that he was, had once managed to talk Pappa into giving us a nice painting of tulips, by a well known Swedish artist. It fit nicely beside the porcelain stove. I did not notice for awhile that the painting was gone. When I asked Urban about it, I did not really get an answer.

Pappa had a collection of old coins on display under a sheet of glass. My mother told me that an old five kronor coin had disappeared after Urban had been there on his own one time. I was very upset. But in every argument we had, he threatened to take the kids. He threatened me, pushed and hit me, and when it was over he would forget everything and he was normal again.

CHAPTER 31

ORSA LAKE

It was summer again, and we were in Orsa. One weekend, Urban had asked an older man if we could borrow his rowboat that was tied up at the beach where we used to go. He said, "Sure, but it has a leak. You have to scoop out water once in a while."

I was not in favour of going out on the lake. We had recently gotten a dog, a pretty blonde Afghan Hound; Amorana was her name. She could not swim! Urban had needed to jump in one time to rescue her. She would not move. The long hair had floated all around her, and she was looking up with big eyes. That was when we learned that not all dogs can swim.

We boarded the rowboat anyway. The three kids, the dog, me, and Urban with the paddles in the middle. Urban wanted to go over to an island that had Stone Age burials. It did not seem too far away.

The kids sat on the bottom of the boat with the dog. I was scooping out the water. It started getting cloudy, and the wind was picking up somewhat. It started raining a bit. The island was farther then we thought, but we finally made it to land.

After about fifteen minutes, Urban wanted to leave. I asked if we could not rather wait until the rain and wind passed. The sky was getting all black, and the wind was getting stronger. We had nothing to be home on time for. We could really stay. Urban said no, we could make it.

We had to board the rowboat again. There was not a soul on that island, nor on the lake that I could see, and I was very scared. I could see on the kids' faces that they didn't want to go out in the increasingly bad weather, either.

The dark clouds were piling up over Orsa. Some light clouds were streaking under the darker clouds, which were turning almost black. I was now terrified.

We finally made it out. The wind was strong and it was raining harder. Urban had a hard time holding the boat steady in the storm.

The waves where high, with whitecaps. The big waves slammed into the boat and sprayed us with water. I looked down in the water and saw, far down in the dark, giant rocks, , all cold and unfriendly. I thought for sure we would be going down to those stones. The kids were crying and calling "Pappa!" They were clinging to whatever they could find, and I was holding onto Pia—she was not even one year old—and trying at the same time to scoop out the water, but it seemed to be coming in from everywhere. The dog, Amorana, was lying flat on the floor, shaking.

My heart was breaking for my little family that I could not even hold onto.

I thought of my mormor, my maternal grandmother, whom I had always thought of as my angel who would keep me from harm. I looked up in the sky, as if I could see her, but the only thing I could see was a black sky.

I prayed. Mormor would have to find a lot of angels to help us through this.

The wind and rain finally died down. Urban dropped the paddles when we come close to shore, and let the waves carry us in. We made it safely to land. We were all soaked through and through. I don't know if Urban had wanted to show how strong he was, or that he was so stupid that it can't even be called stupid, but I could find no words. Without help from the angels we would still be floating around in the black water out there by the rocks.

CHAPTER 32

KIDS' ROOM

When the kids and I arrived home from Orsa at the end of the summer, Urban had surprise waiting for us again. He had divided the height of the bedroom into two levels. "Downstairs" was a playroom with a playhouse, a big blackboard, and a swing, as well as the kids' bed. "Upstairs" was our bedroom. We could not stand up there, but could lie down and sleep. He had made it nice, with short curtains and nice bedding. Everybody that saw it thought it was it was a smart idea.

Life went on. Arguments, fights, love, in that order. I was sure Urban had someone again, he always had it seemed. I had the three kids. Even though Urban took out us to the zoo, to parks, and even on a ship over to Finland one day, he had not changed.

He charmed my parents into giving him another big painting by the same artist as the previous one, which we no longer had. This one was of a naked lady, sitting and holding a pink sheer veil. I cannot explain it, but the painting disappeared, just like the other painting had. Maybe to a pawn shop.

I think my father looked right through Urban. Pappa said he thought that Urban had had a rough childhood. I never told them, or anybody, how frighteningly angry he could become with me. I thought he would see that as a complaint against him, and that for sure he couldn't take I did not know what would happen if I told anyone, and I would rather not find out.

My mother and Urban did not always get along very well. Urban often talked very bad about her. It made me so sad and angry, because she was the one who always helped us. Whenever we were with friends, he always had a new story to tell about how bad my mother was. He was flat out lying. As soon as I tried to say something, he would talk louder. I don't know what our friends believed. I tried to put everything right to my friends, whenever they would ask me if what Urban had said was true. Urban also made us lose friends. He would say something not so good about someone that was not true, but he sounded so trustworthy that I would believe him, and I turned against that person too.

One thing that drove my mother crazy was that Urban had told our friends and acquaintances that he had bought the Orsa cottage and he was going to renovate it. He said he owned the forest around it, and that elks came right to the windows. (It actually happened once.) He invited friends to come up to his cottage and go hunting. But when they said they were going to come, he always had a believable excuse for why they could not come.

The truth is, the cottage is my mother's inheritance from her father. My parents owned it together. Urban always wanted to be seen as the "biggest" one, having the most money. Saying he owned the Orsa cottage was perfect.

And sometimes he was so nice to my mother. Sometimes he would see a dress when we'd be out shopping, and he would say, "That would look very nice on your mother!" And he would buy the dress for her. My mother said he was like Dr. Jekyll and Mr. Hyde.

One day, the kids were with my parents. I was in the new playroom Urban just built them. I don't remember if we had argued, but most likely we had. There was a crack in the window glass. I don't know how it got there. I picked up a doll off the floor. She had light blue pyjamas on. Pia must have forgotten to put it in bed, Thona rather played with trucks. There was still a soft smell of new wood, and I looked over at the playhouse and the blackboard, where one of the kids had been painting.

Urban came in, and I put the doll on the bed, and said to him, "This is such a nice place! You did a great job. The kids love it!"

I looked up, and there he stood with a pistol in his hand! I opened my mouth to say something, but he said, "I am going to shoot you, Birgit." He aimed, and *pop* ... for a second, I thought I was dead.

He must not have aimed directly at me, although in my scared mind, I thought that he had. I stood as if nailed to the floor. I could not believe this was true! That Urban had a pistol and wanted to shoot me! My heart almost stopped.

Urban went out of the room, and seconds later I heard the front door open, then close.

I never saw the pistol again. I didn't dare to ask.

It was all but forgotten, put in the back of my memories.

CHAPTER 33

GOODBYE STOCKHOLM

We baptized Pia at the German Church, a beautiful old church with a tall spire, in the middle of the Old City. It had been built in the 1400s. Once again, Mamma's baptismal gown was in use. Pia was quiet when the minister poured water on her head. Her name was Pia Birgit, and my mother was godmother.

The days went on like usual. One day as I went across the big street to buy our daily groceries, I thought, surely it cannot be meant to always be like this. The door to the grocery store had been locked, because of the drunken old men from the nearby pub that hung out there with their beer and liquor bottles.

Now I had had enough of living here. We had good times with our many friends, and we had a nice home, and that was all okay, but where were we? How would we get further in life? Soon it had to be different.

It looked as if Urban could not found a really good job. He wandered from one small place to another, and his income was never secure. Actually, there was always a question in my mind, whether he gave part of his money to his extra girls. Did he still fool around? It made me very sad sometimes, and angry.

I read the *Dagens Nyheter*, the big daily newspaper in Sweden. Usually I looked for workplaces that were hiring, for Urban, and one day, I could not believe what I saw. A company in America was advertising for furniture cabinet makers. Applicants were to go to Grand Hotel in Stockholm, and the date, time, and room number were provided. There was also a number to call and apply.

I got all excited! I had a hard time convincing Urban, but he called. And we went. There were a lot of applicants in the room. The interview went well, and I thought Urban did his best, and would have a good chance.

It did not take long before we got a letter saying that Urban got the job, along with two others. I was more excited than Urban. We had to sign a paper stating that we were bound to stay with that company for two years. No problem!

Urban had a friend who had a girlfriend in East Germany. He was going to visit her, and asked if Urban would travel with him. Of course Urban said yes. He thought it would be nice to buy the kids clothes there. Kids' clothes where cheap and you paid no tax in the Eastern Bloc.

Urban came home with tons of clothes for the kids. I have to say, they were the prettiest clothes I had seen. For Thona he had bought a double breasted coat. It was blue satin, with the pockets and collar trimmed with red satin, and the coat was lined in red silk. She looked like a princess in it.

We had begun to get the weekend paper, the *Democrat and Chronicle*, from Rochester, where we would live. The newspaper was sent to us so we could see prices and stores, and learn about Rochester, I guess. We had never seen such a big, thick newspaper. And the smell! I stuck my nose right into the paper, and smelled America! I sat for a long while with the newspaper in my arms, and could not believe that we would be soon be going to America.

The company had already gotten us a place to live. The house that they had rented for us was close to work. But so much more had to be done. We had to visit the American Embassy, doctors, get our passports ready, and decide what to do with the apartment and our furniture.

At the Embassy we were asked a lot of questions. Urban was German, he had a German passport, and the kids were German. We were then told what shots we needed for admittance into the United States, and where to get them. And then we were told that we had to be in America before twelve midnight on New Year's Eve. The quota for cabinetmakers had been reached for the next year, they told us. On our last trip to the embassy we got our Green Card.

We also had to tell the tax department that we were leaving. We paid our taxes, and there was two hundred dollars left, for going to America.

My mother didn't know if she should laugh or cry. Pappa definitely cried. The rest of my family, well, I don't know what they thought. Nobody in our family had ever been to the states, and none of our friends had, either. Most of them thought that it was fantastic that we were going. Some, though, thought that we were stupid and daring. We didn't know anybody there, and it was adventurous to go away with three small children. We had no idea what was going to be like. We just knew we had a contract for two years.

A couple of weeks before Christmas we started to sell off our furniture. My Aunt Karin took the pink sheers, raw silk, and the green sofa. I wonder who took the black-and-white cow hides we had on the floor, there were three of them. They had been our carpet; Urban had gotten them as a gift from two farmers in northern Sweden, for getting them work in Stockholm. My parents got the big mirror from the king's house. We had gotten it from Arne's father, who was the tailor for the king's house.

An antique dealer and his family got our apartment off Urban. We did not have to clean it for them, just leave whatever we wanted to leave. Now that I think of it, I am sure that it was the man he sold our "lost" paintings to.

We were leaving a very heavy drawer full of books for the new owner, and it had to be carried up to the storage room on fifth floor. We were on the third floor, and there was no elevator. The stairs were marble, and the drawer was so heavy, I almost could not hold it. Oh yes I could, Urban said. I was going backward up the stairs. I don't know, but I thought it was harder to carry and walk up backward, and that Urban should do it.

On one step, I did not get my foot up fast enough. I thought Urban was going too fast, and pushed me. My foot got stuck between the drawer and the stair, and I fell and hit my bum on the edge of the stair.

I was hurt; I didn't cry, but was not far from it. Urban just said, "Come, we will switch sides." I told him it hurt a lot, but he said I should just carry this drawer up, then we would be finished and I wouldn't have to carry any more.

It did hurt for long time afterward. I felt it for a couple of months. And now I don't know if it was an accident, or did Urban mean to hurt me. Fifty years later, I had an X-ray on my back because of my arthritis. The first thing the doctor said, was, "You have a broken tailbone! You broke it long time ago; how did it happen?" I said I didn't remember, which was actually the truth, but by the time I got home I did remember, but I never told the doctor.

The night before we were to leave for America, we all slept at my parents' place. My parents did not go with us to the airport. Pappa could not take goodbyes, so Mamma and Soffie, the landlord's wife, stood and waved goodbye to us when the taxi took us away.

It was hardest on Pappa. We were his everything, and he thought he might never see us again. A brother of his father had never been heard from him again after they waved goodbye to him on a big American ship that was heading for New York. Nobody knows what happened to him. In that time, people disappeared often to and in America.

My grandmother and Karin, Margit, and Majken, Pappa's sisters, were all at the airport, to say goodbye to us, as well as my girlfriend Maggan and her husband Bengt. There were some teary eyes, and many hugs and kisses.

A flight attendant helped us to our seats with the kids, and off we went, flying higher and higher over Stockholm. And out over the archipelago called *skärgården*. We had made ourselves comfortable, when the captain's voice came over the speaker. He said that we had to land at Copenhagen Airport, Kastrup. There was something wrong with the motor.

My heart jumped. I thought, my God, I hope we make it to Kastrup before one of the propellers dies! I stared at the propellers until we landed. We had to leave the airplane, and go into the hall and wait. We waited for almost two hours before we could go back to our seats in the airplane.

And so it started, on a big SAS propeller plane and two hundred dollars in our pocket. We were on our way to America!

CHAPTER 34

AMERICA

It was late evening, and the plane circling over New York before landing. We were in America! It was breathtaking, and I wanted the feeling of wonder to last forever. My stomach leapt at the sound of the wheels touching the ground. That I didn't pass out from excitement was a wonder in itself.

We went through customs, picked up our luggage, and came out into a big hall. We stood there for a second, not knowing what to do. Then we saw a man holding a sign that said "Ohms Family." We waved and went toward him. Ha smiled, and welcomed us to New York. He said he had been sent by SAS Airlines to bring us to a hotel, because we had missed our connecting flight to Rochester, and that had been the last flight of the day.

The taxi driver brought us to a big hotel called The Roosevelt. The door attendant took our luggage and carried it into the lobby. We went to the front desk, and were told that SAS had put us up in the hotel, and that we would be driven by the same taxi driver to LaGuardia Airport the next morning, where we would get on a flight to Rochester.

We sat down in the lobby, our eyes on a very big Christmas tree. It was trimmed so we could hardly see any green. But the most amazing thing was that the tree was turning around and around as it was playing Christmas songs, and it was snowing on the tree! The kids stared at it with their mouths open. I did, too!

We went up to our room, still in a daze that we were in America, in New York! There was a TV in our room, and Urban turned it on. It was colour! We had never seen a colour TV; the kids where happy.

The next morning our friendly taxi driver drove us out to LaGuardia Airport, where the plane stood that was going to take us to Rochester. LaGuardia was a smaller airport, and as we were waiting, Pia made friends with a little girl who was with her grandparents.

Nobody was there to meet us in Rochester. We had the number of Urban's boss to be, but we could not use the telephone, because we did not understand all the letters on it. The little girl's grandparents looked at us and tried to say something. The grandfather helped us with the telephone. We called the workplace, but it was New Year's Eve, and nobody was working. The grandfather found the address of the workplace, and Urban's new boss was going to meet us there.

He drove us to a woman's house where we could stay over the holidays while she was not home. The woman was a retired schoolteacher, and a friend of the boss. She had a nicely furnished home, and I was not very at ease there, with the kids around all her knickknacks.

After the holidays, the woman took Gunnar and enrolled him in school, and took Thona to kindergarten. In Sweden, children started school at seven years old, in the first grade. There was no kindergarten. That meant that poor Gunnar was in bad shape. He could not understand one word they were saying to him. Thona could not either, but at least she had half a year of kindergarten to learn to speak English.

We had moved into our house. It was empty, except for a big pile of newspapers in one corner of the living room, and a big American refrigerator in the kitchen. There was no heat, no electricity, nothing. We made a bed for the kids in a big American trunk we had borrowed from friends. The kids slept on the clothes that were in the trunk, and we covered them with my red fox fur. We sat on piles of newspapers, which was also what Urban and I and slept on. I was thinking, "we sold the butter, but lost the money," but I was not afraid, not everything was bad. Urban had a job, and the kids were going to school, except for Pia, who was only three years old.

We had to wait until we had saved some money so we could by a kitchen table and chairs. I turned the bottom kitchen drawer, the deepest one, upside down, to use it as table when we ate. We ate off paper plates, because there was no stores around that we had seen that sold any porcelain. There was also not a furniture store in the area.

We had only two hundred dollars to start with, and after paying for rent, gas, and electricity, there was not much left. But we could buy one-day-old Wonder Bread for ten cents!

CHAPTER 35

ROCHESTER

I sat on a pile of newspapers, leaning against the dining room wall. Pia and I needed to go to Star Market, a big grocery store, right across the highway on East Avenue. The word "avenue" reminded me of movies and music, so American!

There was a bridge over the highway, to East Avenue. On the other side of the highway, was a church. It did not have a tower like I was used to seeing on churches, it had a flat roof, with a lot of black birds landing on it. I used to sit and look at them, how they all clumped up beside each other. I could also see Star Market, our nearest grocery store, from the window.

We still had no furniture other than mattresses, pillows, and blankets. Urban got to borrow a Cadillac from a car dealer, and had gone to the Sears store. He loaded the mattresses onto the car's roof, and drove home.

We got a beige carpet for the living room from Urban's work. We had two decoration pieces, gifts when we left Sweden: a gold apple with a long, thin candle, and a Thousand Windows crystal vase. They stood in the middle of the carpet!

The kids shared a bedroom, and all three slept on the same mattress. We had the other bedroom, and we slept on the box spring.

Grocery shopping was not easy. I usually went by the picture on the package. One day we thought we were going to eat something special. It was a package of two cans together, one was big and the second one was much thinner. It looked like the big can would be soup, and the smaller one would be shrimp. We loved shrimp, and I felt so lucky to have found it.

We opened the big can first. We all looked in the can, and it was water! It looked like some grassroots floating in it. Everybody was silent as we opened the one with the shrimp on the can. That had to be good. Urban opened it, and we looked in. It was pink sauce. What was this? We did not understand a thing!

We swallowed our disappointment, and thought at least we would have dessert. It would be a "dessert dinner."

It was a big can, with a piece of apple pie on the picture. So for the third time, the can opener was working. Pia and Thona stood with their paper plates ready. Urban took the cover off; it was white on top. Urban dug deeper in the can, and it was all white.

Both Urban and I put our noses in the can ... it was lard.

So the days went by. Urban liked his work; everybody was nice, and wanted to help. The kids got lots of toys from Urban's work friends.

One day I was sitting on my pile of newspapers as usual. I thought a cat would be nice to have, so I was looking for an ad for free kittens. Instead I found an ad for a monkey. Free to the right family! I felt we were absolutely the right family. How lucky could I get? A monkey!

The owner brought the monkey to us, with a cage. I named him Albert, after my father's middle name. We loved Albert.

It soon started to smell like a "monkey house," so I had to give Albert a bath. I held onto his tail, as I started to wash his hands, then his face. It didn't take long before he was in the bathtub, and loving it. Especially eating the soap!

I took Albert with me to the Star Market. It said "no dogs" on a sign, but I figured Albert is not a dog, so I brought him in. He was sitting on my shoulder. People stared at me! First the cashier said no, I could not bring a monkey into the store. Then they called on the manager. The cashier explained that I was from Sweden and did not talk much English. The manager seemed to like Albert, and he gave him a banana. We walked in every day thereafter.

Rochester was nice. We finally got furniture. We took a taxi to Lauer's Furniture, and we ordered all our furniture. It took long time before we got it, but in the end, everybody was happy.

We also bought our first car. It was an older two-seater Mustang, with a chair-like back seat, where the kids squished in. It was a beautiful car, but it was too small, so we bought a bigger car, a red Pontiac.

I made a friend, Annette. Her daughter Michele was Thonas's best friend from school, and they lived five minutes from us. Annette and all our kids sat in the back seat of the Pontiac when I went for my driver's licence. It was pretty funny, and nobody was allowed to speak, but I got my driver's licence!

I got a job at Neisner's in downtown Rochester in the advertising department as a layout artist. I made another friend, Rosalind, and she and Mars, her boyfriend at the time and later her husband, got together with Urban and me often.

We bought a house in Henrietta, New York. Rosalind and I showed our work at the Clothesline Festival, a big art show in Rochester. It was so nice and fun! I sold quite a few of my paintings and drawings there.

Urban had changed jobs, because the company that had hired him in Rochester was moving to Pennsylvania, and we did not want to move. Pia had started kindergarten, and now all the kids were in school. Urban and I were both working.

Albert could not be left alone in the house, so we gave him to a kids' petting zoo. I think I cried for a week!

Later on, I would have other things to cry over. Urban was not nice to Gunnar. He was really mean, calling him names, and punching him. Urban's mother had come to visit from Germany. Gunnar would be ten years old the day after she left. She left a birthday gift for Gunnar, telling him he could have it on his birthday.

Instead of getting the present, Gunnar got his ears full of not nice words, and his birthday was "deleted." I never got to know what Urban's mother left Gunnar. But probably money, that Urban took.

My cousin from Orsa came to visit us. He was sixteen years old at the time; his name was Ove. Ove wanted very much to get a Winchester Buffalo Bill rifle. Urban located one, and bought it for Ove. Ove stayed with us for three weeks, and when he flew home he had forgotten his rifle.

But Urban hadn't, and one day we argued over nothing as usual, and he ran for the rifle. He pushed me against the wall and threatened to shoot me. I saw Pia from the corner of my eye, she was the only one home. Urban did not shoot me, but he scared me.

Days went on in that fashion. Then the kids got to fly to Sweden for summer vacation, to stay with my parents, their grandmother and grandfather (*mormor* and *morfar* in Swedish). I was so happy that they were going to have the same happy summers that I had as a child. Everything would be beautiful around them and there would be no fights and arguments, only loving hands.

The kids spent three or four summers in Sweden. My parents loved having them there, and the kids loved it. When they were up in Orsa the first summer, each kid got a goat! The next year they each got a bunny. My cousin Åsa had a horse, so they got to ride. A farmer had his cows close by.

I went for a doctor appointment every six months. After one of those appointments I was told to come back and my husband should come with me. I wondered why.

Urban and I went together, and the doctor was very nice. He spoke softly and said I had cancer, and was going to need a hysterectomy. No, I thought, I was not sick, I was healthy, I was anything but sick!

I did not win. I would be having surgery the next week.

On the day of the surgery, I went to work in the morning. At lunch time, I went out and bought a robe and a new nightgown. Then I walked to the hospital; it was not a long walk. As I sat there, waiting for my name to be called, I looked around and saw the other women that were in for the same thing as me, I imagine, and they had their husbands with them. I did not. I thought, why didn't Urban get off work? That bothered me.

I had the surgery, and when I woke up, Urban was sitting there. I felt happy again. I stayed for a week in the Genesee Hospital. Everything went fine, and soon other plans were being made.

Urban had an uncle that was the German consul in Toronto. He thought that Urban and me should move to Toronto, Canada. I did not want to move again. I happened to love my work and my friends here in Rochester. I told Urban he could move, and I would stay here.

Urban went to Toronto several weekends, and I am sure he didn't meet his uncle all those times.

One Sunday I sat outside on the front step, waiting for Urban to come home from Toronto. I looked at my car in the driveway. It had something hanging from under it. I looked again, and it looked as if it was some kind of a tool. Just then Urban came home, and I asked him what that was. He looked and said it looks like somebody had tried to cut the brake line.

Then I figured maybe it's time to move on. We would wait until the kids finished school for the summer, put up the house for sale, and move to Canada. During his weekends in Toronto, Urban had looked a bit for a house, and found one he liked. He had even talked to the owner.

Within a week of putting it up for sale, the house was sold. The moving truck was packed and we were ready to get moving. The rifle stood hidden in a corner of the garage when the moving truck drove out from the driveway.

CHAPTER 36

ENTERING CANADA

Urban, Gunnar, and Thona went in the moving truck, and I drove behind them in our car, with Pia. Gunnar's bicycle was hanging on the back of the truck, so I could easily recognize them, in case I became lost.

At the border, we had to give up our Green Card, a symbol that we were not living in America anymore.

Then we drive on the QEW, which was a long, flat highway. It looked like a moonscape! We passed Hamilton and Burlington, and finally saw a sign for Toronto, Highway 401, but it seemed we were passing Toronto. Not there yet!

I had not seen the house that we had bought before we got there. I thought it must be the White House, it was so expensive. One hundred and twenty-five thousand dollars! Our house in Rochester had only been twenty-three thousand, but the new house was not any bigger than the one we had just left.

Urban had wanted something from a store we had just passed, and as I was going to get it for him. I backed up, and heard a funny noise. It was our TV. I had backed into the TV! Nobody had seen me do it, so I quickly drove around it, and went to the store.

Later, Urban would tell people he packed everything himself and drove to Toronto, and the only thing that was a little bit broken was the TV. He doesn't even know today, that it was not his packing that broke the TV, it was me, with the car!

Urban liked the idea of redoing the kitchen. He put a hole, in the kitchen wall, with a hammer, then the windows. I left for Sweden. I didn't want to live without any windows while he was building. The kids thought it was funny.

When I came home, there was a big, beautiful, bay window in the kitchen. The next projects included redoing the living room, and making the garage into a big studio for me.

We also planted a nice garden, with plants and bushes, and made a rock garden by the basement walk-out.

Meanwhile, I was looking for work again. It was not that easy. I freelanced for Simpsons for a while, but it was long ride into the city.

I found out Scholastic was looking for a layout artist. It was a long road up; we lived in Guildwood, a nice place on the shore of Lake Ontario, and Scholastic was in Richmond Hill.

I had brought a little book I had done, and I showed it, because I didn't have illustrations to show. The art director liked the book, and asked if she could keep it and show the editor. I got a call a week later, saying that they were going to publish the book. I was in my glory! And I was hired, on top of it!

I stayed with Scholastic for one year. The drive to work was long, and I didn't like it as much as I thought I would. The art director and I did not like each other, but I met a friend, named Linda.

After that, I got a job in the advertising department for Kmart, in Brampton. I stayed for about seven years, and made many friends there.

Our marriage was up and down. I went to Sweden alone a couple of summers; I thought I needed that.

Urban was still sleeping around, saying he was going out to meet the guys. Once he went to Rochester to meet with his old friends, and stay overnight. I was glad that he was going to see them again, until we met one of the men and he said, "Oh Urban, that was a shame that you couldn't come. We had such a good time, and everybody asked for you."

There we go again. Urban had told me about everybody he had met there, and how much fun they had, and how the guys had been asking about me and sent their greetings.

That was not the only time he did that. And I was so naïve. He and the boys were going together to watch the Formula F1 car race in Hamilton. It happened to be on my birthday, but I thought that it was a nice idea for him to go.

"Oh, don't worry about it, we can celebrate my birthday when you come home the next day," I said.

So away he went, but not with the guys.

We went to a party sometime afterward. A guy come up to us and said, "Urban where were you that time we were watching the race? We had such a good time!"

Urban is such an expert at lying. Nobody can see through him. Not even me, who was on my guard all the time.

We had sold our car to our neighbour for seven thousand dollars cash, while Urban was in Germany for a week. Urban came home on a Friday evening, and went to work Saturday morning, taking the seven thousand with him. He said he was going to take it to the bank. He was home by lunchtime, crying that he had lost the money. He said he had gone to put some work clothes on, and when he came back, the money was gone.

I wondered then, and still I wonder now, whatever happened to that seven thousand dollars. I was devastated at the time. There were bills to pay. Why had he insisted to be paid in cash? The car, by the way, had been the car I was driving, so technically it had been my car.

We lost good friends because of that. Urban accused the man he had been working with of stealing the money. That was terrible. We were in the same group of friends as he, and we lost them all. But Urban was pretty good at serving up false tears.

Urban and I had many fights during that time. I ran away a few times. I would run to the car, put the girls in, and drive away quickly. Gunnar was usually not home at the time, but one time he got beaten up by Urban. We ran out, calling to Gunnar, but Gunnar stayed. So I drove to the police station, and asked with a shaky voice if they could please send somebody to the house and see if Urban is getting wild. I told them Gunnar was in the house. They promised to drive down and check. Then the police asked me if I had been hit, and I said yes. They asked if I wanted to report him, but I said no.

I drove to the city, to a girlfriend I knew. The girls and I stayed there for a night.

It went like that, off and on. Once the girls and I sat on the cliffs by Guildwood, in the evening sun, again wondering what to do. Other times, I was by myself, sleeping in the car.

Urban had a day off work, and we were driving to the States. Suddenly, he got really angry. He raced other cars, racing all over the street from left to right. I was deathly scared! I said, "Let me drive!" He stopped and got out of the car. I slid in behind the steering wheel, put my foot on the gas, and I was gone! I looked in the rearview mirror, and there he stood, looking at us!

I drove to my girlfriend Annette's place. She and her family had moved from Rochester to Honeoy Falls. I sort of knew the way. We were just outside Buffalo when I started driving. Annette was surprised to see me, and I stayed there for a week.

Thona had gone to Munich over winter, and had learned to ski. She fell in love with the ski teacher, Michi, and his family. Urban invited Michi to visit us. Michi came, and he was really nice. We drove down to Florida with Michi and the two girls for a week's vacation. Gunnar did not want to go.

Thona got a different boyfriend, Bill, and Urban did not like him. Urban dragged me out to the car, holding a kitchen knife, and raced from the driveway to catch Thona when she left work. I don't know what he was going to use the knife for, but he was wild. Thona's boss let her out the back way, and her boyfriend, now her husband, picked her up.

Urban was very generous, and he wanted me to have everything that made me happy. He bought me tons of beautiful clothes. Everything he brought home fit me; I was a perfect size 8 then. But he broke my heart so many times that I was numb.

I had quit my job at Kmart, and got a job with Robinson in Burlington. We had also sold the house and moved to a very nice apartment in Toronto. It was called Sutton Place, and we were on the twenty-ninth floor, with a big balcony.

Thona got married, then Pia got married, and Gunnar moved to Sweden. I figured a new—maybe a nicer—chapter in our life would start.

My God, was I wrong.

CHAPTER 37

TORONTO

A new day and a new life. I stood on the balcony, looking out over Yonge Street. I could see the whole east side all the way to Scarborough and Lake Ontario. It was such a nice view. I liked it, and I felt kind of free.

Our bedroom window faced the balcony and the living room was right beside the balcony. Now we only had to get some chairs and a table and a grass rug for the balcony.

Soon I had painted flowers on the balcony wall, and found a table for my typewriter and put that out there. I had made it nice for myself while Urban went to work. The bedroom was big enough to put the easel in.

I was happy living in the city. I guess I was actually a city kid from the beginning, having grown up in Stockholm. I had quit working. Although I was not really sick, I had rheumatoid arthritis in my hands. I could still paint, and that's what I did.

I thought Urban was happy too, until he started run to the telephone every time it rang. He also started to answer the phone in the bedroom when we were in the kitchen, even though there was a telephone in the kitchen. Once I made an errand in to the bedroom while Urban was on the phone. The conversation quickly changed from a soft whisper to a businesslike voice. Then I knew.

One day Gunnar called from Sweden. He told me that morfar was sick, and in hospital. Gunnar was very distressed, and so was I. Pappa had never been sick. I asked Gunnar if he thought I should come home, and he said he did.

Two days later, Thona, Pia, and I were on an Air Canada flight to Frankfurt where we changed to an SAS flight direct to Stockholm. Mamma met us at the Arlanda airport. We hugged, and of course there were tears. We were happy to be there, and Mamma looked the same, but it felt strange that Pappa wasn't there as well.

The next morning, we went to the hospital. It was very close, so we just walked there. Gunnar had driven down from Orsa to meet us, and Pappa, their morfar.

Pappa was very happy to see us all, but I could see that he was getting tired quickly. He that usually was so alert. His doctor came in and asked if I was the daughter, and said she wanted to speak to me. What does that mean? She told me that Pappa had cancer in his pancreas and that it had spread to his liver. And that he had only two to four weeks more to live. She had told my mother, but my mother had not seemed to understand.

Pappa had been coming home from bowling and had dropped in to his doctor's office on the way home to get the results from the blood test he had done a week earlier. The doctor had sent him directly to the hospital.

Pappa was in hospice for two weeks. I was sitting by his side when he passed away. I had been stroking his head and telling him how much I loved him. He took his last breath while I still was talking.

Thona and Pia had gone home a week earlier.

After the funeral, I wanted to go home, but Mamma wanted to keep me as long as possible. She did not get me a ticket to Frankfurt, and I had to stay for five weeks.

I got a strange feeling when I walked through the door of our Toronto home. Urban always wanted our home to be nice and clean, and it was. But there was no "welcome home sweetheart." I was not happy.

I went to unpack, talking about the funeral. Urban had asked me to tell Pappa that he loved him, I told him that I had said that. I opened my underwear drawer, and the first thing I saw was underwear that didn't belong to me. I paused, and said, "This is not mine." I don't remember what the answer was, or I don't want to remember.

Urban sent me down to the office. He said he had left the keys outside the door, and now they were gone, and his office keys had been on the chain. What a liar. He did not forget the keys, the girl had keys to the apartment! Now he wants another lock so she can't drop in all of a sudden while I am there. He is such a coward!

We got a new lock.

A few days later, the telephone rang, and I answered.

A child's voice said, "Can I speak to Chevette, please?"

"There is no one here with that name," I said.

"Is this not number so-and-so?"

"Yes."

"Chevette told me she would be with Mr. Ohms, and that I can call her there."

I was stunned. I said, "Chevette is probably out shopping. You can reach her at her home later."

My heart stood still for a second. Then I took a paper and wrote Urban a note. I wrote that a little girl had called, and asked for a Chevette. I wrote that I told the girl Chevette was out shopping, but that she can come back and stay with Urban. I am gone. Sincerely, Birgit.

I called my son-in-law, and asked if he could pick me up after his work was finished that afternoon. He said yes, and he picked me up at the coffee shop around the corner.

When I returned a week later, I met the cleaner on the twenty-ninth floor. He came and hugged me and said,

"Mrs. Ohms, I thought you had left! I have seen this young girl going in and out of your apartment." I told him that was just a friend of ours. I felt ill.

Urban came home, and I had made a painting for him. I was going to save it for his birthday, but I felt that maybe I wouldn't get him anything. I showed him the water colour, and he thought it was so nice. Until I told him what it meant.

There was a woman's face in the foreground. Beside it, in the background, were two big, black birds. The face was supposed to be me, and the black birds were birds that destroy other birds' nests. The black birds were Urban and Chevette.

It did not go over very well. Urban took the painting and ripped it to pieces. I had been prepared for that, and had taken a photo on the painting, so it was saved anyway. That was actually the first time he had harmed any of my work. He usually wants to see my paintings, and encourages me.

By this time, I was so angry, I could spit nails. But it was not over yet.

I went to my doctor, who sent me to a gynaecologist. I went to the appointment, had some tests done, and got a prescription for some pills for me and my husband to take. The problem I had did not go away, so I went back to the gynaecologist.

I don't remember if it was the same evening or shortly thereafter, but I was surprised when the doctor called me at nine at night. He said I should call his nurse and set up an appointment.

So I called the next day, and got an appointment the following day.

The doctor called me into his office, and closed the door behind me. He told me to sit down, and we talked about some common things. Then he said I had a virus I could only have gotten through intercourse.

He said, "You or your husband has been getting it from somebody else, and carried it to you. The next stage is herpes."

I wanted to disappear! I thought I might suddenly break down and cry. I don't know how I made it out of the office, only that the doctor was very nice, and said some sweet words.

I got home and told Urban, and we both got a pill to take.

I also found about a hundred photos of Chevette that Urban had taken and thought he had hidden well. In one photo she was sitting in the car, holding up her hand with a ring on it. It was my ring with the big turquoise that I thought had gone missing. In other photos, she was wearing my furs in restaurants in the city, and even in bed.

My stupid husband; he fifty-six years old, and she is nineteen or twenty! She is only with him as long as she will get all these things from him. My God, how stupid can you get? And I thought that he was so intelligent.

He once said to me, "She does what I tell her to do."

I said, "I heard she works at McDonalds, that's a future to be proud of. I also heard she got fired from there!"

I was so mad, I was shaking.

Urban wanted us to buy a little summerhouse where we could go for the weekends. I thought, no way would he get another "hacienda." We would buy a house far away, with neighbours that they can see us coming and going, and also see if somebody else is coming and going.

It was just as well. Sutton Place, our apartment building, was for sale, and we, the renters, had to find other apartments. Some people had been there since Sutton Place was built.

We did not get what Urban wanted. This time, we got what I wanted. A house far from the city, in Pontypool. We had never heard of it.

Pia and I packed and did most of the moving. Urban was busy saying goodbye to his girlfriend Chevette. They sure wouldn't be able to see each other that often anymore, and she could not live with

Urban. By the way, I heard she was getting married. I wonder what her husband would have said, if he had known.

It seemed that I was always moving away from something. This time it was to a big house far from the city. My whole life, I seemed to be fighting for being the only one for my husband. He was not even breathtakingly handsome or anything like that. He was just not a very ordinary guy.

And now, hopefully, the last move. I sure was beginning to get tired of moving. But little did I know, what more was in store for me.

CHAPTER 38

STRENGTHENING OUR VOWS

But first we had to celebrate that everything was good again. That we loved each other, and that we always had and always will. I thought, *it can be discussed ...*

So at the breakfast table one morning, I drew on a napkin the ring that I wanted. Urban added the diamonds and the things to finish it off. He took the napkin to a goldsmith he knew, to make the ring.

The ring was beautiful, exactly what I wanted my wedding band to look like. We were going to marry again, this time around in a church. But which church? "In Munich, naturally!" Urban said. "No, in Starnberg, where I was baptized!"

Yes! Starnberg was a pretty town, not far from Munich. We were going to Munich anyway, it had already been planned. Now we had the ring, and hopefully the church too, and we were going to "strengthen our vows." The year was 1999.

We arrived in Munich and informed Urban's mother about the marriage idea. She thought it was splendid. We went to Starnberg, a little town an hour from Munich. We went to the church and got to talk with the priest, and the wedding was in the making.

We stayed at Cafe Berg, which was a restaurant and hotel. It was really Bavarian, many guests were dressed in lederhosen and dirndl, German folk dress.

Our room had a balcony overlooking the Bavarian Alps, a beautiful view! It was a very romantic place.

Our wedding was pretty, and there were more friends there than we had counted on. Mother had told a lot of our friends.

Our friends, Dieter and Brigitte, had picked us up with their car that had a banner with flowers for us. They also had a surprise for us when we came out from the church. They had put a white tablecloth over the side of some stairs, and put out a lot of glasses and champagne! Music from a cassette in a car was playing the "Wiener Waltz." Urban and I had our wedding dance on the parking lot in the sunshine, with champagne glasses in our hands and our friends all around us. That was a beautiful moment!

We had thought we would go to a simple little place after the wedding, and eat potato soup, like the old times. But with so many people at the wedding, that would be a problem. Urban took a chance and called a place, a beautiful restaurant not far away from where he used to live. Sprengenöder Alm, it was called, it was an old timber house, high up on the mountain, with a wonderful view of the Bavarian Alps.

The restaurant had everything ready for us in a bit over an hour. A wedding table, flowers, candles, and everything. So we all went, including the priest.

It was a very nice dinner, and the food was delicious. Everybody was happy, even though they had never heard about "strengthening the vows."

CHAPTER 39

PONTYPOOL

Now Urban could carry me over the threshold! That's what I had always dreamed of. I had chosen the house in Pontypool, and Urban had redone the whole house, both inside and outside. It was going to be a house where the sun was always shining.

I painted a lot, and I wrote many letters to friends. No one had email. Urban and I still argued, though maybe not as much as we used to.

We were up early every morning, because Urban had to leave for work at 4:30 a.m. He had a long drive to work. I was not sure if Chevette was still around some place.

Urban often had to travel for work for longer times. He asked me all the time if I wanted to go with him, but I was a bit careful, thinking about what would happen if he would start fighting with me, for example in China or Japan, where would I go? I did not go with him that often. I stayed home with my cats. I also had some friends, and Thona lived close by.

But Urban would soon have a problem with Thona and her family. He found everything that was wrong, and told everyone how bad she and her husband were. Urban treated our friends the same way, he was lying through his teeth. Then all of a sudden, everything was good again, for Urban. I cannot even tell you how things turned upside down. So much for the sun always shining!

I was going to be sixty years old, and I did not want to have a big party. I did not want to invite many people, but I didn't know exactly what to do.

Urban said, "We are going to celebrate your sixtieth birthday at Stockholm City Hall, where they have the Nobel Banquet! You can have dinner there and you get the Nobel Prize dinner from whichever year you wish, it's like a menu. Karin, your aunt, can ask about it."

We flew over to Stockholm. My relatives, and friends, even those from Munich, came to the party. Nobody had ever eaten at City Hall. That was something special.

The china, glasses, and cutlery were all from the same year as the chosen dinner. It was just a beautiful place. I got another surprise, a friend, Rudolph, came down the stairs, playing "Happy Birthday" on the saxophone!

Soon after, there was another important date. It was the new year of 2000! This occasion was going to be celebrated in Sprengenöder Alm, where we had the wedding dinner. We had had already reserved a room in the Bergs hotel, where we had stayed for our wedding. It would be a formal, festive night, and the people that would be attending were many upper class and aristocracy.

Evening came, and people made their way through mountains of snow walls. It was already dark and cold, and the stars were bright. We parked the car on a hill. Farther down the hill, were some snowy wooden stairs. It was hard to manage in high heels!

There were beautiful people, and those who thought they were beautiful; it was a very happy atmosphere. Everybody stood with a glass of champagne, and everybody was talking with each other. I did not know anybody, but Urban knew some people. But that didn't matter, we were in a group and everybody talked to me. We were the only "foreigners," for lack of a better word. The food and drinks were wonderful, the dessert was great, and so were all the people.

When it was time to greet the new year, we all took our coats, and went outside on the big patio. There they had a bar made of ice! Everybody got a glass of champagne, to be ready for a toast when the church bells rang in the New Year 2000.

All heads were turned toward the mountains. It was a beautiful night. The sky was a canopy filled with stars. It was cold, but with the dark was all around us hugging us like we were in a dark blanket, it felt warmer.

The church bells rang and the fireworks started all around in the villages beneath us. We toasted, and it was a happy feeling to ring in the new year.

CHAPTER 40

HOME AGAIN

For years, I have gone to the doctor for my rheumatoid arteritis
Urban always drove me. This time, we came home, and when I got
out of the car, suddenly I could not stay up. I tried and tried, and
finally I stood up and walked, but it was like walking on a boat. I
could not walk normally. Urban called the hospital and they said he
should bring me in.

I looked up at the ceiling in the hospital room. I turned my
head and saw some treetops. I didn't get it. I'd had a stroke. The
stroke affected me on my right side, and again, I had problems with
walking. Pia came and took me out in a wheelchair, and she drove
me so fast that my hair was flying in the wind as she took the corners
on two wheels! It was funny!

I was home a week later. But soon after, my right knee started
hurting very much. So much that I could not stand it anymore.

We saw a surgeon, who, to our big surprise, said he could do a
knee replacement surgery this Sunday morning. Sunday morning
came, and I got a new knee. So now I had a steel knee! Well that's a
durable thing! Three days later, I got to go home.

A therapist came a few times, to help me use my knee, but I could
never stand on my knee again.

Back in Stockholm, Mamma had moved to a home for older people. She was fine, and had it good. She had her own furniture and paintings in her room. We had gone there when she turned ninety. There was a little party in the dining room for her.

One day we got a call from a nurse at the home, telling us that Mamma was not good; actually, they thought that she was dying. We told them we would be there right away, tomorrow, or the next day. Well, we came too late.

Mamma had passed away that same night.

After the funeral, we had to empty the apartment, where Mamma and Pappa had lived for fifty-five years. Thanks to my girlfriend and her husband, the man that played saxophone on my birthday, we got the whole household moved out the before the first of the month, and the apartment cleaned. We took some stuff to the Stockholm City Auction. Friends took some things, we sent some up to Orsa, and gave some to the Salvation Army. It was very, very hard.

That was so much work, and Urban was sick, so he didn't help. That's where I first saw how Urban was playing sick. It had not been so clear before. He was sick, with heart failure and myasthenia graves, but those things do not made him that sick. Our friends and I were working our hearts out. And Urban was just lying on the sofa and was too sick to do anything.

"Sick"? He was not too sick when it came to checking out my parents' drawers and papers!

I got funny blisters under one breast. I thought my bra had not been rinsed out well enough, but then I thought, how come on one side only? Urban was too sick to go with me to the walk-in clinic, so I went on my own. The doctor looked at me, and said it was shingles. That was something awful. I don't know how I got it, but probably because I had been under stress.

CHAPTER 41

ONGOING STROKE

I didn't like the way Urban was reacting to things. It was as if life was only all about him. One morning, felt the same as I had when I had the stroke. I told Urban and we waited to se if it would go away, But it didn't

Urban had called Pia, who lived in Aurora. She came and met us at the Bayview Hospital Emergency. The nurse told us I had an "ongoing stroke." The doctor sent me home, and I got worse. Urban called Pia to come and drive me back to the hospital. He said he was too sick to drive. But Pia, who had been up for twenty-four hours, she could drive!

She made the one-hour drive from Aurora, then drove me back to the hospital. By this time I could hardly speak.

I lay in the hospital for ten days, not being able to move or speak. Then I was taken to the Toronto rehabilitation institute on University where I stayed for four week

I had to learn how to speak, move, stand up, walk with a walker, and eat. When I came home, life was as usual, except that I could not do anything anymore.

The last time we were in Orsa, I was walking with my walker and I felt weak all over. I passed out in the grass, and I remember Urban standing over me, saying, "Stop your theatrics. Stand up!"

I went to see my doctor the day after we got home from Orsa, to find out why I was so weak. He did some blood work .After that, I wanted to go and get my hair done, so I called for an appointment and got one for the next day.

Before I left for the hairdresser, I fell on the bathroom floor, and threw up orange juice. I said to Urban that I didn't want to go and have my hair done because I didn't feel good. But Urban said I had to go, because I would feel better when I had nice hair.

My hairdresser said out loud, "How can you have orange juice in your hair?"

When we got home, we saw my doctor had called me three times. I returned his call, and he said I had to go to the hospital right away, because I needed blood.

I needed three bags of blood. But not even there would Urban stay with me. No, he had not brought his pills with him, he said it was necessary for him to go home and take his medicine. Thona stayed.

CHAPTER 42

NOT FUN

Living with Urban was not any fun anymore. Urban was so mad one day, I went to hide in the closet. When I came out, he pushed me so I fell on my elbow, on the stone floor. I must have broken it, it hurt so much. It still does when I touch it on a specific point.

Then he wanted to sell some gold. It was all organized in a drawer, with some in jewellery boxes, and some loose. He took out the drawer and took all boxes and loose things out and put them on the sofa. There he played with all the things: chains, bracelets, rings … every day. I was so sick of seeing him playing with the gold, and I knew he wanted to sell some of it, things that I didn't use. I told him to go ahead and sell what he wanted. So he did. Mostly they were things that my mother had worn.

Urban was acting slightly strange sometimes; he was more violent. One day we were driving, and a whole line of cyclists merged from a side lane. They had the right of way, but Urban pushed on the pedal and hit the last biker in the line. Urban looked different.He stared straight forward,and bit he's teeth together .He looked like a dog that was going to bite !

The young man was mad at Urban. Urban said that the bike had hit the car. I knew that Urban had swerved right into the guy.

The police stopped us, saying that a young man on a bike had been hit by this car. The police officer was a woman. Urban to sweet talked her, saying that she surely knew how kids were, they had to make it the car's fault, because they needed something replaced on their bike.

Nothing was wrong with our car, and Urban left as the gentleman he pretended he was.

Another time we were waiting behind a school bus that had stopped. Urban thought he had waited there long enough (too close, if truth be told), so he started to drive before the stop arm was in and the stairs were folded back in.

The police came to our door later. Urban had to go to court. A few weeks later, Urban went before a judge. After all this, Urban won again! The bus driver that charged him was apparently wrong. There is no limit to Urban's innocence!

It made me almost happy to hear that Urban wanted to sell the house and move to the city. I had started to worry; where would I be able to go if I needed help? Nobody would even hear me here if I should have a problem with Urban. And I knew it was going to come, I could feel it.

There had been too much of that lately, him saying he or she had stolen things from him. He had been too sick to drive me to Peterborough for my rehab twice a week; Pia drove me. It took her a whole day, driving and waiting. Urban had even gotten for real, so sick that the doctors had called us to talk to us, because they thought he was dying. Twice! But that had not changed him a bit. He was not grateful to get another chance at life. Now, he started where he had left off.

There were so many things he blamed on old friends and new friends. I constantly had to defend friends and the kids, and he disliked them more and more. He told Thona when she came visiting one day, "I don't want to see you anymore. I can look at a picture of you. That's good enough."

We sold the house, and I thought we lost a lot of money on it. Urban was not a businessman. He would rather give things away. He had already given away a great deal of our furniture and other things to strangers, just so none of our kids would get it. That's not a sign of a loving father.

This year would be our fifty-fifth wedding anniversary. And I thought to myself, "Is it meant to be like this my whole life? What was the meaning of it? What have I done that was so bad? Why was I saved in that bike accident, and Kjell not? Was I not good to Urban? Is it partly my fault that our life has turned out like it has?"

CHAPTER 43

BLOOR, BAY, AND YORKVILLE

Another move. This time we went back to the city, to Toronto, on Bloor Street East beside the Hotel Plaza II. Well, that was central enough.

The apartment was a one bedroom, with an interesting open concept, renovated by the former renter. It was on the twenty-eighth floor, and there was no balcony. It had a north view, which was not bad, but there was no sun. But there was an elevator, so when the sun came around, I could go out.

The apartment was nice. Urban even fastened handles for me, spaced evenly along the walls so I could walk holding on to the handles.

It was also easy to get to the plaza underground, to stores like The Bay and Shoppers Drug Mart, and some other stores. We lived practically on top of the stores; it was great.

The apartment was too small for all our things, so we had to rent a storage space. Pia rented it for us in Port Perry. At the time, Urban was too angry to pay for storage, so Pia paid.

When we left Pontypool, we had bought a little puppy, a Shitzu ,she was the quietest thing! We named her Chichi, and Urban loved the puppy. Chichi went with us everywhere.

I was walking with my walker outside one day, and I was worried about walking as far as Urban wanted me to. I knew I was not strong enough, but he wanted me to cross Yonge Street. Urban got irritated when I didn't go fast enough. There was a green light for us to cross the street, and I told him I couldn't go that far. He said I could, and told me to go. I started to go, but when I came to the middle of the street, Urban told me to go faster, because the cars were coming. The light was changing, and I panicked and froze. Urban left me to go to the other side. He left me stranded in the middle of the street, with the cars waiting to go. Since then, I didn't want to go out with Urban with the walker anymore. I sat in the wheelchair, with Chichi on my lap.

One day we went out like that, I in my wheelchair, Chichi on my lap. There was construction in front of Holt Renfrew where they were making space for taxis and cars to stop to let customers in or out of the cars.

The sidewalk made a bow inward, and Urban claimed he hadn't seen that. He went straight out. The wheelchair tipped over, I fell out, and Chichi was on the street. In less than a second, there were many men around me, helping me up. They carried me to my wheelchair that somebody had put on the sidewalk again. They ran after Chichi, and Urban could get up himself. I was not hurt.

I was hoping it was an accident, but I knew it wasn't.

I was starting to feel trapped where we lived. There was nobody in the office after six o'clock, and nobody was there on weekends. There was no security guard, nothing. I could not manage getting out on my own, because the stairs had no handrails. I did not feel safe.

We had been looking at apartments on the corner of Bay and Bloor. The building was secure; it had a concierge, and a valet who took your car to the garage and helped with your bags, if you needed. They were there twenty-four hours a day, seven days a week. There were no numbers on the doors, and lots of people. I really wanted to move there.

The apartment we looked at was also one bedroom, with a balcony overlooking Bay Street, facing east. I liked it. Urban was not so sure about moving, but I was. The longer we lived on Bloor, the more thoughtful I got. I felt it was not good there.

I would have liked to talk about it to any of the doctors I saw. But no, Urban sat in on every appointment I had. Actually, he had done so ever since I had stroke. There was no way for me to speak with anybody, without Urban being right there. Sometimes, when we would be waiting for friends to come visiting, he would tell me I should not say anything, that he would talk. So, I just spoke when I was asked to.

I was pretty quiet anyway. I did not have anything to say when Urban was on his "high horse." When he would say he was a world traveller (he was not), or that he had been in every country (he had not). Urban always had to be the best in everything. Except, he admitted, that he was not very good at plumbing!

However, every time I needed help, he was always there to help. He did the cooking and the laundry. He showered me, and washed my hair. He dressed me when I couldn't do it. He combed my hair and put it in a ponytail. He cleaned me after I used the toilet. And he took care of Chichi.

On the other hand, he could get more than furious. It was scary, when he got like that, frothing at the mouth. And lately he had been starting to threaten me that it would be a bloody ending, and I should call my girls to pick me up. But when I reached for the phone, he wouldn't let me call.

I was pressing for a move to Minto Yorkville, so we moved. It was more security in Minto. I felt safer there, then as Urban now was I could feel that something was coming

That was our second move in a year, and it was tiring. The move was just around the corner, but the things, like furniture and rugs, kept piling up on us.

In the end we had to rent two storage spaces in the building, and the rest went to the other storage unit in Port Perry.

We soon had made friends with almost all the employees at Minto Yorkville. I made friends with a woman named Christine, she was a massage therapist. I got a massage once a week. Christine looked like Audrey Hepburn. She was slim with short black hair, tucked behind her ears. She often wore a men's straw hat and a thin black coat. She had a white poodle, Oliver, that was always with her.

I got a personal support worker. She showered me, and then we walked outside on the sidewalk. She was very nice, but Urban had something against her, so I got a new one. That one would later steal my bracelets. I was furious! My first gold bracelet that Urban had bought me in Sweden, a wide x-link, and two 24 karat gold arm rings from Mecca were gone.

Urban had started showing his strange side. He really lost it one time when we were in Shoppers Drug Mart on Bay Street. He threw the things that he had in his hands into a basket that had some sale stuff in it, and started pushing the wheelchair quickly out of the store. I tried to put my feet down, to stop the wheelchair. But he was furious! I thought, should I scream? But that would probably make it worse.

Outside the store, I put my feet down to break his speed, but he pushed the wheelchair straight out, over the sidewalk. He paused, waiting for the traffic to come. I still had my feet on the ground, and Urban was so angry that he sounded like a dog that was going to bite. And then, out of nowhere, came a young man. He approached Urban and said, "If you go a bit farther, there is a traffic light. I will go with you and show you."

Urban went back to normal, and thanked him.

We went home, saying nothing.

CHAPTER 44

IS THIS THE END?

Urban did not talk to the kids, anymore, and he did not allow me to, either. He did not talk very nicely about any of them, or about their families. And I was, of course, to think the same. Urban had me under complete control. I don't know why he had such a sudden hatred toward the kids. They had never asked for anything, they had always only been there to help if we asked.

I never complained to the kids. They saw things for themselves. I guess I had always lived by the saying, "You've make your bed, now you have to lie in it." Now I was just wondering how it was going to end.

I was uneasy, and I felt that something might be coming up. Things as they were right now could not go on forever. It just had to reach an end.

Urban started accusing me of taking things, that I had no idea about. One day we were in the kitchen and he turned around to me holding, his favourite knife. It had a yellow handle, we had gotten in Sweden.

He held up the knife and said, "It's going to be very bloody, if you don't watch it," and he pointed the knife at me. "Where is the copper kettle? That I inherited from Mammá. Where did you hide it? Or have you given it to the girls? Where is it!!"

We had left the copper kettle in Orsa, but he would do this with different things, at different times. Mostly they were things we didn't have anymore.

I had to know where the kettle was in ten minutes. Or else … he showed me the knife. I was very scared. Nobody would hear me if I called out. The next door neighbours were friendly, but they were often gone during the day. Chichi was afraid.

Then Urban said, "Get dressed, we're going out for a walk." Urban never went alone for a walk with the dog. Oh no, I had to come, whether I wanted or not. We usually went to the little park beside the old fire station on Yorkville. We spoke to the fire guys a bit, and let Chichi run loose in the park. We were usually out for one or two hours.

This time he went down the street, by the restaurant where no dogs were allowed. We turned the corner, and went toward "our" espresso café, but Urban went by. We were not to the corner yet, when Urban suddenly increased his speed, and almost ran. A taxi cab was about to turn at Bellair and Cumberland, and Urban rushed diagonally across the street. I thought he was going to drive me right into the taxi.

And bang! Urban hit the front wheel of the taxi. The taxi driver jumped out, and was so afraid that he had hit me in my wheelchair. He said he was so sorry, he had not seen us. I was stunned! Had Urban really tried to kill me, or just scare me? I had no scratches anywhere, other than on my heart.

Urban talked to the taxi driver, to calm him down. But he told the driver to look out when he was driving. This time, Urban said, nothing had happened, but next time maybe he wouldn't be that lucky. Urban gave the driver a friendly pat on the back, smiled, and said goodbye.

Urban and I did not say one word about it. We went by Starbucks on the corner of Bay Street, and Urban asked me if I would like a coffee, and I said yes.

I did not dare mention anything about what had just happened. We had our coffee, surrounded by the noise of other people. When we got home, I went directly to bed.

I would usually wake up between one and two a.m. every night, and tell Urban I would like coffee and a cheese sandwich. He always got up right away, and made that for me. This night I did not wake up, and the next morning was like every other morning. The day was nothing special. I was only worried about what might be. And I didn't have to wait long.

Evening came, and bedtime. Urban asked me for my jewellery that I wore every day. I had just been taking it off, and I said, "Here it is," and put it on the bed.

"All of it," he said, "the rings, too."

I gave him the rings. He turned around and put everything in a plastic bag.

Morning come quickly. It was the third of December, and I had a hairdresser appointment, just in the Manual life Centre.

But that was not on Urbans mind. He asked me where was my jewellery.

I said, "I gave it to you last night."

"No," he said, "I don't have it. Where is it?"

I said, "You took it and put it in a plastic bag, and hung it on the chair."

"It's not there. You have hidden it!"

"I cannot walk to the chair. How could I hide it?"

Urban went to the kitchen and said, "I give you ten minutes to give me the jewellery!" He pulled open the cutlery drawer, and took out the yellow knife. He turned to me, and waved with the knife.

I said, "I don't have it; I don't know where it is. I gave it to you, and maybe you have forgotten where you put the bag."

As if that would him get to think. No, he got angrier. "I will turn this drawer upside down, so tell me where it is!"

I said, "I don't know."

And bang! There went the drawer and all the things fell out on the floor.

I thought, I don't want to show how scared I am. If I can just act as if I have everything under control and stay calm, maybe he will calm down.

But no. He took a Meissen cup, showed it to me and said, "Are you giving me the jewellery, or not? I am dropping this Meissen cup!"

I said, "You have it, I don't know where it is."

Crash! There went the Meissen cup.

The Meissen porcelain is very important to Urban. Germans are showing their wealth when they can afford to buy Meissen. It must have broken his heart to smash a Meissen cup!

I left the kitchen area, but Urban came after me, and stopped at the small cabinet where we had all the sterling cutlery.

"Tell me where you have it!"

"I don't know."

"I'm going to put all this in the garbage!"

Now he started to sound really threatening. He went and sat down in a chair, waving the knife at me and talking about a bloody ending.

I really did not know what had happened to the plastic bag of jewellery. Urban got angrier. He was pulling out the big desk drawers where all the important papers and photos were. Everything was on the floor.

Again he sat down, and said, "See, I am going to drop this, if you don't tell me!" It was the big Meissen floor vase, of which Urban was proud.

And smash! The vase broke. Now he was really heated. I stood there with my walker. Urban came closer, with the knife. And I thought, is he really going to kill me? Is this the last chance I have? Should I scream? And I did.

"Help! Help!!"

His hand quickly covered my mouth. "I'm going to tape your mouth! Where is the big tape?" I knew where the tape was, I just hoped he did not remember. He pushed me to the side, with my walker, and I fell.

I tried to move, but I could not move a thing. I was in excruciating pain.

"Urban, can you help me?"

"No." Urban had returned to his chair.

"Can you call downstairs, to the concierge, and ask if somebody can come up and help you?"

"No."

The person that I knew was not there. Urban was a stranger, with no emotions, showing no expression in his face. His eyes looked like ice. He just sat there, waving his knife. Then he stood up, came to me, and pointed the knife at me, touched my hand with the tip of the knife.

I lay there for three hours. I told him that I had to go to the bathroom. He said, "Yes, go." I pleaded with him to call an ambulance, or ask the concierge to call a paramedic; I said I could not lie there forever.

He called the ambulance.

CHAPTER 45

GETTING A CODE

Urban had picked everything up, and put it all in drawers, so nothing was left on the floor. There was a banging at the door, and the ambulance attendants came in. The two men were very nice, but when they found out that I had been lying there for three hours, they were a bit questioning.

"Why did you not call earlier?" They asked Urban. Urban answered that I did not want him to help me, and that we had slept for a while. I don't think they believed his explanation.

I let out a scream when they moved me onto the stretcher. It hurt tremendously.

Then Urban wanted go with the ambulance, him and Chichi! I don't remember what excuse he gave, but they got to sit beside the driver. Urban was not allowed to sit with me.

We got to Toronto General, Urban and Chichi in tow. I had a broken hip. The doctor asked how it had happened, did Urban push me? My answer to that was very vague. I knew my answer should have been yes, but I didn't dare say that. I thought, then what is going to happen when I go home again?

I was told that I would have surgery in a day or two, and asked whether I would like to go into rehabilitation after the surgery. Urban thought I would not want to do that. He said he could take care of me. Urban was surprised when I said I would like to go to rehab.

I was taken to my room, which was the smallest room I've ever seen. There was not much to look at out the window, just another uninteresting building, but the window sill was full of beautiful flowers. Only now do I know why I was put in that room. It was because I had the nurses' station right outside my room, in case Urban should try do something. At the time I did not know that.

The surgery went well, but that does not mean it didn't hurt afterward. It did. I was really angry at Urban. Because of him, I had to go through all this pain.

Urban was there every day. The kids thought they would give him a break, and all come to see me on a certain day so Urban could take a rest.

Urban stayed in that little room and sat beside me, on the only chair. He was there while the girls visited me. I hardly got to say a word, and they could not talk freely to me, either.

When they had to go home, Caprie, our granddaughter, asked if she could drive Urban home. He said yes. It was really very bad of Urban, to sit there like a statue when the girls came to see me. I thought it probably was so I could not say anything bad about him.

And that's not all, in the bad behaviour department!

Urban had a few loud arguments with the head nurse of the department. Urban was not allowed to take Chichi into the ward. The nurse said she was going to throw them both out, and called the security on Urban. I was ashamed.

Finally, after close to two weeks, I was moved to Bridgepoint rehab. There I also was put into a room close to the nurses' station. The room had two beds and a big bathroom with a shower. Each patient that I shared the room with had also had hip surgery. I stayed for three months, the longest time anybody could stay there.

On one of the first days I was in rehab, Urban came in with a big smile, saying, "Look what I found!" He took a little bag out of his pocket, and there was my jewellery. He said he had forgotten he had put it there, but wasn't it nice that he had found it?

I was not amused! I got so angry! He had put me through all this pain and agony. Not only me, but the kids and our friends, too. I just could not smile. I just wanted not to be there.

Urban was there every single day, rain or shine. He was allowed to bring Chichi with him into the ward. Pia and Thona had to call me before they came to visit, so they would not interfere with Urban's visit. Urban did not want to see any of the kids, so he was careful to not meet any of them. Urban called and asked if they, Pia mostly, were there, and for how long. Then he came afterward. Urban would get very angry if they showed up without him knowing. He would monitor everything we said, and it was stressful all the time. I don't know how many times I was reminded that the father of our children hated them.

The nurses and the doctor was very nice. Every second day I had training, or stretching for my legs. I noticed I had been regressed since my first rehab, when I had the stroke. I was hoping I would be as good as I was before I ended up here.

On the twenty-third of December, the whole family came to have Christmas with me. There was a big room in the rehab centre where we could have company, and it was so nice! Urban came after they had left. He always wanted to know what the kids had been saying. He always thought we had been talking about

Thona, Pia, and I had been asked to see a special nurse. She asked us what Urban was like, and asked me if he had pushed me when I fell. I gave her a little better answer, because I was now feeling more safe.

I said, "I think he lightly gave me a push, so I lost my balance and fell over the walker." I was not able to say, "Yes, he pushed me!" Then what would happen to me when I went back home?

What I didn't know at the time, was that as soon as any nurse looked up my name on the computer, there was a red flag attached to it. That was a warning against Urban.

The doctor asked me a couple of times if my husband was a narcissist. I said no. I thought the doctor had a different way of saying "Nazi," and I knew Urban was not a Nazi! I had never heard the word narcissist. Not even Pia knew when I asked her.

Now I know that Urban is a narcissist. After fifty-five years, I finally had a word that described his behaviour. For that I am very grateful to my doctor. Even though I did not understand him at first, he gave us something to wonder about, and to finally get an answer. Since then I have read many books on narcissism.

But it didn't end there. My stay in rehab was coming to an end. I had been able to go home for a couple of weekends, and it had not been as fun as I thought it would be. Now the doctor had reluctantly given Urban permission to take me home. I think even the personnel were a bit worried. I was.

The last day I was at rehab, Pia was visiting early, before the time Urban usually came, which was two o'clock. Urban called, and he was not happy. He got more and more aggravated, and started yelling on the phone. I got tired of listening, so I gave the phone to Pia. Urban went on screaming at her, saying that he hated her, and was going to kill her and her whole family. He said he had already made everybody's coffins!

I was so afraid to go home. Pia had left, and Urban came. The nurses kept Urban busy for the longest time, speaking to him and asking him questions. He did not look as happy as usual. We left rehab without saying goodbye. Urban went fast, with me in the wheelchair, to the elevator, and then to the car. I was really afraid to go home, but unless it showed on my face, I did not tell anybody.

When I got home, I called Pia. She said we have to have a code, so I could call or message her if Urban got violent again. She said they would be there in no time. She said she would sleep by the phone, and I could call anytime. Urban hated her, so she could not call me at home.

We made a code that I could use with either the phone or the iPad. I hoped it would all be alright, and I would not have to use the code.

I was lucky to have had the code.

CHAPTER 46

THE POLICE

Urban did not seem to be very happy that I was home. Sometimes I thought he was happy, but he went back and forth, and nothing was like before.

One morning, on the fifth day that I was home, he started arguing with me. I don't remember why, but he said that he was going to send me back from where I came. Meaning rehab.

I said, "They won't take me, I have been there for the longest time I can be there."

"Then you call your daughters, and they can take care of you!"

I said okay, and he threw me the phone, from the bedroom to the bathroom, but it landed far away from me, and I could not reach it. He was getting heated up, why, I didn't know, but I felt something was brewing. I couldn't get him back to being normally sweet and friendly. He did not even look like I knew him.

I was worried. I got out of the bathroom, and he went in. He yelled something from the bathroom. My heart was pounding, and I looked at my iPad, which was beside me. I thought this was probably my only chance before he takes my iPad, so I cannot contact anybody. I remembered one scary morning when he had taken my iPad, threw it someplace, and ripped out the telephone jacks. This time he had forgotten to take the iPad away. I quickly opened it, looked for Pia's name, and entered the short code.

Urban came out from the bathroom, and was saying something, when the phone rang. It was Thona. She said she was on her way to the city, and wondered if there was something Pappa wanted or needed. No, there was not, he told her.

Soon thereafter, Gunnar called! He and Urban talked, but they were suddenly interrupted by a loud banging on the door.

"POLICE! Open the door!"

My heart was in my throat. I thought, Pia! She got my code! Urban was wearing only his underwear, so he quickly put on jeans, and opened the door. At once, the apartment was full of police. There were five big guys and one woman, who came in to me in the bedroom.

The police said that there had been a lot of yelling, so the neighbour had called the police. Urban turned to me and asked if he had yelled, and I said yes. But that was something the police had made up, to give a reason for why they came.

They went into the kitchen. Urban stood by the drawer with the knife in it. He seemed absolutely normal. The police asked him questions. They where just waiting for him to make a wrong move so they could take him.

Thona came, and Urban talked to her. Pia was outside in the hall, but the police had told her not to go in, because she had told them Urban hated her.

The talk between Urban and police got heated. Suddenly, Urban opened the drawer that he had been leaning against. He quickly got hold of the knife, held it up to his throat and screamed it was going to be bloody!

The police were there in half a second, and took the knife from his hand. He didn't even see where it came from. He pulled away from the police, and made a run for his pills.

A fight broke out, and the police won. They handcuffed Urban. He pled with me to come with him. But I told him the police were just going to help him. Thona quickly took me out in my wheelchair. She didn't want me to see my husband getting led away to the police car

Thona and Pia drove me to the police station. There, we were each interviewed, and it took the longest time. The waiting was awful. We were there until midnight.

Thona and her husband Bill took me home to their house. This was to be my new home.

Urban was held for a week, I think. I do not know exactly what was happening with him, but he was given many tests. A psychologist came and saw him every week. Urban was issued a restraining order for a year, to protect me and the kids.

This whole thing has been put very much stress on Thona and Pia. Gunnar is living in Sweden, and I don't know how he is with his father. I am reluctant to say Urban's name to my sons-in-law.

It has now been three years since that happened. I have met Urban twice for coffee in a café, together with Pia and my granddaughter, Caprie.

Urban had not changed. Was I married to this man?

EPILOGUE

Many times I have wondered why I was saved in that motorcycle accident when I was fifteen. Exactly five years later, my cousin died in the same kind of accident. He had also been fifteen. Was my life already mapped out? Was my purpose to write, so that I would teach other women to not fall into the same trap as I did?

My hope is that young women will read this and realize what can happen if you are not prepared, and don't follow your instincts.

It would also make me happy if you would look up narcissist and sociopath. They can go hand in hand, and there are many people around like that.

I feel good coming out about my story. My hope is that you have learned from it. Then my life has been worthwhile!

CPSIA information can be obtained
at www.ICGtesting.com
Printed in the USA
LVHW112355010620
656229LV00007B/56/J